Digital Media and Risk Culture in China's Financial Markets

This book analyzes the risk cultures in China that have emerged from the entanglement of new communication technologies and financial markets, examining the role that digital media play in Asian modernity and offering an alternative narrative to that of the West. The book illustrates the impact of exclusively Chinese digital media on power dynamics within risk definition, arguing that information and communication technologies (ICTs) empower individuals, enabling them to compete with an expert-oriented risk culture controlled by Government- and banker-led media outlets. With struggles, competitions, compromises, and confrontations, major communicators in financial world are collectively producing risk cultures based on interpersonal relations instead of contractual obligations, in which insider information is valued over professional analysis. Meanwhile, investors are trapped in a risk culture paradox that they themselves have produced, as they attempt to take advantage of other actors' uncertainties and eventually produce risks for the entire market.

Zhifei Mao is an Assistant Professor in the School of Mass Communication at Shenzhen University, China. She was invited to the research team for the European Research Council project "Methodological Cosmopolitanism – In the Laboratory of Climate Change" led by Professor Ulrich Beck from Ludwig Maximilian University of Munich as a postdoctoral fellow. Later she worked as a postdoctoral fellow in the School of Journalism and Communication, the Chinese University of Hong Kong. Her research interests are in global risk, environmental communication, new media studies, and financial communication.

Routledge Research in Digital Media and Culture in Asia
Edited by Dal Yong Jin, Simon Fraser University

Chinese Social Media
Social, Cultural, and Political Implications
Edited by Mike Kent, Katie Ellis, and Jian Xu

Digital Media and Risk Culture in China's Financial Markets
Zhifei Mao

Digital Media and
Risk Culture in China's
Financial Markets

Zhifei Mao

Routledge
Taylor & Francis Group

LONDON AND NEW YORK

First published 2019 by Routledge

2 Park Square, Milton Park, Abingdon, Oxfordshire OX14 4RN
52 Vanderbilt Avenue, New York, NY 10017

*Routledge is an imprint of the Taylor & Francis Group,
an informa business*

First issued in paperback 2020

Library of Congress Cataloging-in-Publication Data
Names: Mao, Zhifei, 1951– author.
Title: Digital media and risk culture in China's financial
markets / Zhifei Mao.
Description: New York, NY: Routledge, 2018. |
Series: Routledge research in digital media and culture in
Asia; 2 | Includes bibliographical references and index.
Identifiers: LCCN 2018043495
Subjects: LCSH: Capital market—China. |
Electronic trading of securities—China. |
Financial risk—China. | Finance—Information technology—
China. | Digital media—China.
Classification: LCC HG5782 .M378 2018 |
DDC 332/.04150951—dc23
LC record available at https://lccn.loc.gov/2018043495

ISBN: 978-1-138-89583-6 (hbk)
ISBN: 978-0-367-66350-6 (pbk)

Typeset in Sabon
by codeMantra

Contents

Acknowledgments

I would like to take this chance to express my thanks to all the participants of my research of China's stock markets, from those fund managers, government officials, stock commentators, journalists, and editors, to the numerous small investors who shared with me generously their special experiences in the financial world. Some investors are so kind to let me follow them to their homes and working places for observation. Without their help, I could not have approached the construction of financial risk on the individual level.

I would like to thank the book editor, Professor Dal Yong Jin, and my Ph.D. supervisor, Professor Saskia Witteborn, for all of their support and encouragement. And I would like to thank Professor Jack Qiu Linchuan, who shares with me his insights on the issue of class, personal relations, and political economy related to China's society. I also appreciate the help from the financial experts like Zhou Xunyu, Professor at Columbia University, and Alex Preda, Professor at King's College London. Many thanks go to Professor Scott Lash, too, who has introduced risk culture as a concept in his impressive work.

I would like to thank Professor Ulrich Beck, who had invited me into the team of his global project of risk and discussed with me his insightful ideas about risk from the field of sociology. His risk society theory has inspired me to examine financial risk at the very beginning. And I would like to thank Mr. Albert Gröber and all the team members of Professor Beck's project for their great supports and encouragements.

I would like to thank my family members who are always there for me. Special thanks to my parents, Zhou Xue and Mao Zhongqin—their unwavering trust, support, and love are the very source of energy of mine. I would like to thank my dearest husband and son, too, who give me great support and happiness all the time.

1 Digital Media and Risk Cultures—An Introduction

It was 11:05 am on August 16, 2013. Numbers on a big digital screen suddenly started turning red[1] in a stock exchange hall located in the western part of Shanghai, China. Within minutes, the Shanghai Stock Exchange (SSE) Composite Index soared 5.96%. A crowd of people began shouting, most of them small investors or so-called *sanhu*.[2] "What is going on here?" "Anyone got any information?" "The government has decided to save the stock market; I told you so!" "I am going to buy some more stocks and follow the big bankers (*zhuangjia*).[3] It's our chance."[4]

This chaotic scene continued as people began making phone calls, gathering in groups, and surfing the Internet with their cell phones and iPads. Mr. Huang, a small investor in his fifties, recalled that he was among the ones who turned to the Internet for help: "Online sources are full of rumors. But anyway, the Internet is far faster than TV in delivering real-time information, so we looked online to find the truth (about the sudden market surge)." Another participant in my research shared a similar experience:

> It was totally chaotic, a mess, I mean it. Rumors were anywhere. We tried hard to find out what was going on, if it was a great chance or a risky trap. Some investors in my exchange hall truly believed that there was really good news about to be released, and they bought a lot of stocks that day.

Meanwhile, online commentators posted thousands of microblogs about the unusual upsurge in stock prices on the biggest social network site in China, Sina Weibo. The sharp increase seemed to come out of nowhere. Some people suspected that the surge resulted from some sort of mechanical problem in the financial transaction system. Others believed that the Chinese government was preparing to release some game-changing policies that would stimulate the market. Xia, a university student majoring in business management, was in his computer class when this event occurred. He busily checked people's messages on his smartphone and tried to trade stocks using his app, all while cautiously avoiding the professor's attention.

He wrote a post on his own Sina Weibo account that morning with excitement: "Damn it, the market's crazy. I am in, guys."

At 11:47 am, the SSE declared that "the system of the Shanghai Exchange is absolutely normal" on its official Sina microblog. In Mr. Huang's stock exchange hall, an investor shared this news with others only a few minutes later after its release. When officials made statements, they simply ruled out the possibility of a technical error in the transactions. The small investors in the hall, including Huang, were over the moon. "Because the officials said so, we thought, at the time, that it was legit. There must be some great chance coming," Huang said. He and many other investors prepared to invest more money in the afternoon. Xia, however, started to have some doubts: "I wasn't totally buying it. The crucial issue was what the big investors would do in the next step." He tried to keep his cool while continuing to surf the net seeking alternatives to the SSE's claim.

At around 12:30 am, one small investor in the stock exchange hall announced that he had heard from a friend by cell phone that the unexpected surge in stock prices resulted from a brokerage firm's mistake. The name of the firm is Everbright, which is a listed company in China's stock market. According to the hearsay, the firm had accidentally invested a large amount of money into the stock market. Two other small investors who were online supported his claim, finding the same piece of information. Despite the lingering doubt, "many investors in the hall still believed other rumors. Not many people believed it to be a threat at that moment," Huang explained. Meanwhile, using his smartphone, Xia located the exact same piece of information, which already had been reposted many times. He was impressed by the rarity of such "unambiguous information that named the exact company clearly, the Weibo account of which was an official media outlet. I was not sure at that time … but it was alarming, of course." He withdrew from his initial enthusiasm and no longer considered putting all of his money in the market.

When the stock market reopened at 1:00 pm, officials from SSE confirmed that Everbright Securities stock had been forcefully suspended. At the same moment, the firm admitted they made a technical mistake, announcing that it had purchased a huge amount of stock shares due to a mechanical problem in its trading software. The Shanghai stock index plummeted nearly 100 points between 1:00 pm and 3:00 pm. Huang told me,

> I lost 5,000 CNY in a day because of this. My pension is over 2,000 CNY per month, and my wife was angry… A woman in the hall cursed like crazy because she thought the increase in the index was because of some good news, and then bought a lot of stocks in the morning. We small *sanhu* are always getting played and being hurt.

As another small investor, Xia agreed that surviving in China's stock market is hard, but he believes the battle can be won with a good strategy. "The crucial thing is not to trust anyone easily," said Xia,

> Do not trust the listed companies. Do not trust the media. Do not trust the stock commentators. Be smart and careful, look through every piece of information cautiously before making up your mind ... *Sanhu*'s information sources are worse than 'bankers', for sure, but there are still good chances.

Mr. Chen is a big investor, or as Chinese people say, he is a "banker" (*zhuangjia*) who has engaged in financial investments for many years. He had a very different interpretation and experience of the Everbright crisis from that day when compared to Huang and Xia:

> Look, the data showed that it was just not right. The trend (of the stock index) was very strange. It was not normal, not the way a sane banker would trade. If you are a professional, like me, you could tell. I thought it was dangerous to trade stocks at that time, and I phoned some of my friends who worked in this field and discussed it with them ... They had good information sources.

Another big investor who worked as a fund manager was also a step ahead of the small investors:

> I believed that I knew something was not right before the (small) investors knew. We have our ways. After I knew that it was because of the Everbright Securities accident, we quickly came up with strategies to protect our fund from the dangers by calculating future market trends (...) But anyway, I have to admit that we still lost money in the crash. This kind of unpredictable risk is not welcome at all, for it increases uncertainties and chaos in the market. Even if someone won some easy money in this case, it is still highly risky because winning or losing depends on luck, not analysis. And you will probably lose in most cases.

This dramatic event in China reveals the interesting power dynamics among different actors in finance, encompassing the trust issues resulting from the strong government, the grassroots struggles of small investors, and the dominant groups' strategies of defense to maintain their positions. As a communication researcher, I am most interested in this event because of the crucial role that digital media played in reshaping the power relations of financial risk. On the one hand, information and communication technologies (ICTs) triggered a financial crash, causing insecurity and uncertainty instead of reducing them. It's hard to imagine that a goliath market in China would be shaken to such an extent—not by a powerful government's policy or a true economic disaster, but by a single "fat-finger error" in ICTs.

Meanwhile, during this event, digital media facilitated almost every *communication practice* (Couldry, 2004; Craig, 2006), the sayings and doings (Schatzki, 2010) of risk communication. Different actors from the finance community responded to the uncertain event by questioning, chatting, accusing, and analyzing, using the various communication technologies at hand to transform uncertainty into security. The information flow was intensive, the meanings of risk varied, and the power relations in finance became complicated. In the Everbright financial crash, it seems the big investors nailed it in communicating financial risk. They were definitely the experienced and professional ones, and more importantly, they had stronger social capital in acquiring and interpreting information. As the big investors pointed out, their "friends" or "contacts" were instrumental during this financial disaster, granting them swift and secure information. The small investors and the government itself might suspect that this so-called friendship results from big investors' *guanxi*[5] composed of more informed individuals and institutes—potential communicators of insider information. Theoretically, in this situation, there is no way for *sanhu* to compete with the big bankers in risk communication. Only another mighty giant, the Chinese government, can step in and take the lead. But the financial world in China is far more than a clash of the titans. Despite being the obvious underdog, the small investors use their own communication strategies to make sense of crisis situations, using ICT as a weapon. They continue to voice their opinions about the financial markets on different cyber platforms, or comment on and evaluate the experts. They joke, mock, and engage in self-effacing chatter. They refuse to excuse themselves from the games, and sometimes, they even succeed in making a difference in risk communication in China.

Why is this the case, and what are the consequences? To understand the full picture, we need to take a look at the investors' practices in risk communication. When trying to make sense of the uncertain situation, investors use a particular platform or turn to a particular person, among all other options when it comes to information sources. It appears to me that these choices are patterned instead of random, as if these actors are following some collectively agreed-upon norms and rules. In this book, such norms and rules related to risk communication are called *risk cultures* (Lash, 2000). These norms define what language we use when communicating risk, which practice to choose in an uncertain moment, and when to trust or distrust someone. In China, I argue, digital technologies play a crucial part in facilitating very unique risk cultures that differ from those in "more mature" markets.

"Professional West?" Media and Expert-Oriented Risk Cultures

But before jumping into the specific cases of risk cultures in finance, we may take a step back to look at a big picture of risk first. When the dark side of modernity gradually comes to light, the general public starts to voice their own opinions about the risks introduced by modernization. These perspectives, in many cases, depart from the experts' claims (Beck, 1992). There exists a breaking down of hierarchy in defining risk in many contexts, especially during grassroots social movements regarding environmental problems and health issues (e.g. Freudenberg & Steinsapir, 1991; Foster, 1998; Rome, 2003; Nieusma, 2011). The once silent minority groups within a risk community have tended to be the biggest victims of manufactured hazards. Their own crisis experiences have made them experts on risk (Johnson & Ranco, 2011), and they are therefore no longer willing to follow instructions from big brother, big capital, or big academia. They have faced one major obstacle to their grassroots protests, however: the mass media system. The ownership of mass communication technologies (e.g. satellite TV) was centralized, and the cost to build a mass media platform was beyond activists' grasp. In an authoritarian country, the mass media system is, at core, a propaganda machine for the government; meanwhile, in a liberal society, it unavoidably falls under the influence of big capitalists and their political representatives (McQuail, 1994; Humphreys, 1996; Sparks & Reading, 1997). Either way, grassroots movements have had little room to talk about risk in front of a mass audience, and even if they had such a platform, the mass media could discredit their voices as radical and irrational.

The distribution of ICTs seems to have turned the tables, providing more fertile soil to green movements and other from-the-ground-up populist efforts. The government and corporations maintain control, but in the era of digital media, individuals can use a one-to-many media platform at virtually no cost (Dominick, 2010), expressing their own thoughts on catastrophes instead of being overshadowed by elites. In some extreme cases, grassroots activists have taken the lead in communicating risk, searching for reasons and ascribing responsibility (Yang & Calhoun, 2007; Johnson & Ranco, 2011).

Unlike other social dimensions, however, the financial sector seems almost immune to such transformations in risk communication. In most "mature" capitalist nations, the discursive power rests on the shoulders of so-called professionals when it comes to finance issues. Indeed, any news reported on issues related to finance remain tightly controlled by, or given in the name of, professionals. Experts from government departments, banks, and finance companies take it for granted that they should be making judgments and predictions about financial risk. Ordinary people, on the other hand, have no way of claiming a seat at boardroom and policy-making tables, nor do they own any outlet for expressing their thoughts on these government policies or professional analyses.

Why is the hierarchy of financial communication so untouchable? What separates the general public from a position enabling them to define financial risk? I argue that one important reason behind this phenomenon is the particular *risk culture* (Lash, 2000) of finance. It entitles certain expert individuals, institutions, and economic entities privileged positions in defining risk. In this book, I define *risk cultures* as the norms, beliefs, and rules that the actors of a risk community voluntarily or involuntarily agree upon. These norms emerge from the everyday communication practices of different social actors, in turn guiding risk communication in the specific communities of risk. From fund managers to financial news reporters, from economists to law and policy makers, the actors with the loudest voices repeatedly assert that financial risk is somehow "imbued with the image of science" (Bell & Mayerfeld, 1999, p. 2). This discourse forms the legal basis of expert-oriented risk cultures, a claim that insists that financial risk and the financial system in general are too complex to be handled by ordinary people, who are irrational and unprofessional. Instead, financial situations should be and must be described, communicated, and solved by rational and professional *determinate judges* (Lash, 2000) or *expert systems* (Giddens, 1994, 2013). This belief rests at the core of expert-oriented risk cultures; in essence, it is what Bell and Mayerfeld (1999) called the scientific rationalization of risk, a process through which experts apply knowledge to transform the unknown and the uncertain into clear probabilities. Here, knowledge consists of particular languages, models, formulas, and concepts. By communicating such knowledge, *expert systems* exclude ordinary people—or even experts from other fields—from engaging in the communication process. When risk is calculated using a formula or model, its social meanings are eliminated, and only mathematical meanings remain. Suddenly, it becomes "calculated risk" (Abolafia, 2001, p. 29) based not on the rationality of the investors who take the risk but on the economists who measure it.

Obviously, the dominance of this expert-oriented risk culture has roots in other social organs, all of which have faced several confrontations. Some of these contests have moved from the ground up, as we can see in the populism of the green movements discussed above. Meanwhile, some experts have responded to calls from the general public, jointly challenging the existing dominant risk definers. These dominant structures include the government, the big capitalists, and even their own colleagues and institutions (Frickel, 2004 & 2011; McCormick, 2007). In the post-Silent Spring era, these scientist activists have collaborated with local communities and NGOs to confront various risk issues (Mazur, 1998; Kaiser, 2000). Interestingly, the activities of these new players continue to be questioned, especially by their expert peers, some of whom consider them to be biased. Despite such critiques, their very existence democratically shakes the foundation of the knowledge hierarchies inherent to risk definition.

Such revolution from within, however, first requires a common ground for the professionals and the nonexperts, a social consensus of what is right and what is wrong. In the case of green movements, the common good clearly resides in the public good, a mutual sense shared between people that environmental assaults put lives at risk. Most importantly, people need to agree that such risks are not compensable, that they are not simply necessary costs of normal social progress. Ulrich Beck used the term "non-compensability" to describe this kind of agreement on risk:

> [...] the security dream of first modernity was based on the scientific utopia of making the unsafe consequences and dangers of decisions ever more controllable; accidents could occur, as long as and because they were considered compensable. If the climate has changed irreversibly, if progress in human genetics makes irreversible interventions in human existence possible, if terrorist groups already have weapons of mass destruction available to them, then it is too late. Given this new quality of 'threats to humanity'—argues Francois Ewald—the logic of compensation breaks down and is replaced by the principle of precaution through prevention. Not only is prevention taking precedence over compensation, we are also trying to anticipate and prevent risks whose existence has not been proven.
>
> (Beck, 2006, p. 334)

Public agreement regarding the non-compensability of risk has legalized a more equalized and democratic risk culture in some social dimensions, but not in finance: The reason is simple: financial risk or uncertainty is not regarded as non-compensable at all. Instead, it's a combination of chance and loss. This principle holds true when it comes to wealth, excitement, greed, and even pleasure. Because of this bittersweet characteristic, the hazardous part of financial risk becomes highly individualized—it seems "fair" for the individual to take on the risk of seeking additional profits, instead of blaming someone else for causing their losses. As this example shows, the common ground that experts and ordinary people share in the green movement does not extend to the financial world. There is one obvious phenomenon that truly illustrates the difference between finance and other risk issues: Few NGOs are involved in dealing with risk related to financial transactions, because financial investment never tends to be regarded as a public good. Rather, it is all about personal choice.

What are the consequences of the dominance of expert-oriented risk cultures in finance? In my opinion, it poses two problems for financial communities and human societies in general: The first is that the complexity of expert systems may actually produce new risk while attempting to alleviate it (Lash, 2000). A case in point is the worldwide economic crisis following 2007. Did the expert systems in the capitalist world really take the correct actions to ameliorate the crisis, or did they instead deepen it? This question is still subject to debate. Another example will be discussed in greater detail in Chapter 4, the *circuit breaker crash* in China's stock market. In that case, experts and policy makers in China mimicked the trading curb policy (Harris, 1998) of the United States and other more mature financial markets, setting up rules to terminate market transactions during extraordinary stock crashes. They intended to apply such professional tools in order to reduce stock market volatility to avoid a major market drop or panic. Against the expert system's good will, the circuit breaker policy triggered a serious financial crash in China.

Expert-dominant risk cultures present another social problem in their inequality levels. Ostensibly, the issue of social inequality always lies in the distribution of wealth, but in the financial world, the politics of wealth distribution is actually about unequal risk distribution—the latter of which is largely determined by how risk is defined. According to social scientists, risk often has been defined and staged in a way that suits the definers' own interests, causing losses to others (e.g. Beck, 1992, 2006, 2009; Adam & van Loon, 2000). Expert-oriented risk cultures guarantee the dominance of professionals in defining and staging risk. They essentially legitimize a process allowing an extremely small number of people to analyze, to answer, to order, to convince, and even to joke; meanwhile, for the majority of others, their role is to listen, to consult, to ask, and to follow. In other words, risk cultures support the *communication practices* of certain players when defining risk while discouraging others from doing the same. Some of these communication practices occur at the microlevel, like a fund manager telling their clients what to do with their money, or a trader buying or selling a certain stock. Others construct more macrolevel dialogue around financial situations such as when economists discuss economic crises on TV, or in blogs and newspapers. In the name of expertise, big capital and big brother can silence media expressions related to risk that run contrary to their own privileges or interests. Ulrich Beck called this process the formula of *schweigen entgiftet* (silent decontaminates), ensuring the ignorance of risk of the unprivileged groups (Beck, 2009, p. 8). As Chakravartty and Schiller (2010) pointed out, the big bankers can determine when a financial crisis ends through the neoliberal media they control at will. And when such discourse about crises is spread, it becomes true, indifferent to what ordinary people think and experience. Interestingly, in the world of finance, the *schweigen entgiftet* is not just about silencing risk through communication, but extends to chance as well. For example, it is important for market manipulators to keep the public unaware of a devalued stock, so they can bottom fish it with a decent price.

Given that risk communication is so crucial in maintaining these unequal risk cultures, an important question arises: did digital media—believed to fundamentally flip the media power dynamics—ultimately change the game as they have nourished grassroots activities in other social dimensions? Here, I would bring Occupy Wall Street into the discussion, a social movement triggered by the economic crises and other political problems. Suffering from unemployment and pay cuts, people in the United States participated in social protests against wealth inequality, social corruption, and the believed collusion between large corporations and the government financial services sector. Researchers have celebrated the role that social media plays in facilitating such movements (e.g. Gaby & Caren, 2012; Conover et al., 2013), not only promoting the organizations and expanding the movements' scale, but also avoiding traditional media gatekeepers' *schweigen entgiftet* that would have silenced grassroots' voices and other civic debates.

Nonetheless, this massive movement ended with emptiness, leaving no fundamental change institutionally or legally. Only hashtags and pictures on social media still show the protestors' initial hope and optimism. After the movement, theories emerged to explain the failure of Occupy Wall Street, pointing a finger at its loose organization (Pauwels, 2015). I argue that one important reason the movement bore no fruit is that from its very beginning, it targeted wealth distribution on the surface instead of the risk distribution hidden underneath; it questioned the justice of the financial world instead of the professionalism that nourishes the injustice. Thus, the online and offline protests both failed to shake the unwavering risk culture that sustains the dominant position of Wall Streeters and policy makers in defining financial risk. Of course, these financial analysts and policy makers are not on the exact same side with no internal differences regarding risk (as an example, one might reflect on the argument between advocates of the efficient markets hypothesis and the discipline of behavioral economics, or the debates between the liberalists and supporters of government expert system). However, they share the common ground of the expert-oriented culture together, believing that risk can and should be measured, calculated, and solved professionally. This belief, ironically, might be shared by the street protesters as well. All they sought was for the professionals to deal with the economic crisis in a more just way. But what if it is the experts themselves that cause the inequality and injustice? It is like changing a flag to save a sinking vessel.

For me, compared to the Occupy Wall Street protest, a more solid blow to the financial expert system of Wall Street was dealt by Spotify.

This megalith digital media company chose to go public through a direct listing instead of a traditional initial public offering (IPO). To put it more simply, a company usually goes public with the assistance of banks' underwriting, the process of which not only helps to stabilize the company's stock price, but more importantly, serves as a roadshow to global investors. This process seeks to convince investors worldwide that a company is worthy of investment, based on the assurances of financial experts. Companies often pay a fortune for this service offered by finance companies, the dominant risk definers of the financial world. And that explains why the majority of companies choosing to list directly are small ones or startups who could not afford the costs of the underwriters. It remains extremely unusual for a leading figure like Spotify to skip the traditional IPO process, leaving the mouths of hungry finance companies open. Any finance company would love to list a service like Spotify in its annual financial statements. Daniel Ek, the founder and CEO of Spotify, explained their choice of going public as follows:

> Spotify is not raising capital, and our shareholders and employees have been free to buy and sell our stock for years. So while tomorrow puts us on a bigger stage, it doesn't change who we are, what we are about, or how we operate. [...] Normally, companies ring bells. Normally, companies spend their day doing interviews on the trading floor touting why their stock is a good investment. Normally, companies don't pursue a direct listing. While I appreciate that this path makes sense for most, Spotify has never been a normal kind of company. As I mentioned during our Investor Day, our focus isn't on the initial splash. Instead, we will be working on trying to build, plan, and imagine for the long term.[6]

We can see from this declaration that Spotify is a specific case in many ways. For example, the company already boasted a strong subscriber base and fame all over the world before going public. But still, the risk definers on Wall Street might not be happy that a company has found a way around the system. What if other companies with big names and huge subscriber bases follow the path of Spotify? What if more digital tech industry giants stop relying on the risk-defining work of the finance companies? Could ICTs change the risk culture of the West in surprising new ways?

"Irrational East?" Controversial Risk Cultures in China's Stock Market

Researchers definitely should keep a keen eye on what's happening with regard to the questions posed above. That being said, Spotify remains a unique case, at most a glimmering possibility that could trigger future change. Strong as it is, the expert-oriented risk culture in the financial world faces other very real threats. Surprisingly, these threats come not from social activists fighting for public good, but from the "greedy and unprofessional" masses. Some individual investors attempt to step in and take control of the risk management of their own money, crossing the barrier of expertise. For the experts, those investors' communication practices are simply labeled "noise" that interferes with the professional process of risk communication (e.g. DeLong et al., 1987; Kupiec, 1996). As Werner FM De Bondt (1998, p. 832), a founder of behavioral finance, wrote in his famous article "A portrait of the individual investor": "It is part of Wall Street folklore that small individual investors are 'dumb'". In the expert-oriented risk culture, the "dumb" investors are merely the irrational speculators who always suffer from financial crashes and who are placed in unprivileged positions in risk communication. It is not surprising to see that the portion of individual investors is comparatively low in those "more mature" financial markets in the Northern America and Europe.

Are the hierarchical relations in risk communication the same in Asia? A crucial difference between those young Asian markets and the ones in the West with long histories is the significantly larger portion of individual investors such as in China (Ng & Wu, 2010), Korea (Chung, Lee, & Park, 2014), Japan (Japanese Statistics Bureau, 2017), and Taiwan (Barber et al., 2009). These investors refuse to trust their assets to professional experts and instead control their own capital. Following the logic of expert-oriented risk culture, one can declare that this characteristic is the result of the youth, immaturity, and even the amateur status of many Asian financial markets. Government experts claim that these individual investors' intervention in the professional communication of risk causes high volatility and chaos in the financial markets. The only solution, it seems, is to shift to the dominance of expert-oriented risk culture and exclude these investors from risk communication. During my interview with a high-ranking officer at the Hong Kong Stock Exchange (which is regarded as a more mature and liberal entity among the Asian markets), he advised that allowing institutions to handle stock investment is a more effective way for Asian investors to avoid suffering: "Go for mutual funds—investing in individual stocks, unless you are wealthy enough to afford a diversified portfolio, is usually not a wise strategy for individuals" (high-ranking officer at the Hong Kong Exchange, interview, June 4, 2013).

In the specific context of China, the government has heavily promoted professionalism through state-oriented newspapers, radio channels, TV programs, and other forms by mass communication. It has disseminated professional policies, economic statements, and financial analysis, officially calling for a more stable market guided by experts. The government also exercises control over the expert system through the licensing mechanism. Only those who pass government examinations may call themselves stock commentators or analysts, sharing their opinions as experts in the media. Mainstream media outlets repeat a famous Chinese saying, "The stock market is risky. Be cautious when entering the market"—warning people to follow expertise and not engage in gambling-like speculation; otherwise, they will suffer.

Contrary to the government's good will, though, excessive speculation is so common in China that investors use the term "stir-frying stocks" (*chaogupiao*) more frequently than "investing in stocks" (*touzigupiao*) to reflect trading practices that are short term, unstable, and are price oriented instead of value oriented (Gamble, 1997; Kang, Liu, & Ni, 2002; Green, 2003). Big bankers manipulate the market at will by using their capital to collude with government officers, listed corporations, or experts so that they privately gain insider information, spread false information through public media, and then bait small investors. Small investors, on the other hand, have deep distrust toward licensed experts. In a famous financial fraud case in China, small investors rather followed blogger Daitoudage777,[7] who had little educational background in finance and experience in dealing with risks, instead of relying on the analysis of professional experts on TV (Du, 2007). The seemingly almost "barbarian" and gambling-like risk culture has dismantled professionalism in financial markets in China. Consequently, such risk culture resulted in the failure of government attempts at centralizing norms and beliefs with regard to risk communication.

Why Digital Media Matters: A Digital Form of Occupying Wall Street in China

One might argue that the risk culture in China hurts the reputation of the financial markets as a whole. With the country to be the economically gigantic, Shanghai and Shenzhen should be representing wealth and chance in the eyes of financial investors worldwide. However, they also signify chaos, bubbles, fraud, and instability for the experts, ironically, just like the outdated term "shanghai" used to be defined in the 1800s English dictionary. Hundred years ago, "to shanghai" in English means drugging and kidnapping people to be sailors. The denial of expert-oriented risk culture seems to allow the financial markets in Shanghai to "shanghai" many small investors. But if we look at this phenomenon from the perspective of risk communication, we may see that these Chinese individuals have maneuvered into more powerful positions in risk definition than their Western counterparts, and they are able to compete with experts in communicating financial risk. It was not the case before the widespread use of digital media in China. In 1990s, the Chinese government once tightly controlled financial markets through state-oriented mass media in the name of expertise. For example, on December 16,

1996, a newspaper article titled "The proper understanding of the stock market" was published in *People's Daily*, the mouthpiece of the Chinese government. The author of the article accused both big and small investors as irrational and expressed that the surge in the market was merely excessive speculation. The market immediately crashed after the article was published, with numerous investors selling their securities out, the index of which dumped about one-third. About two decades later, however, after *People's Daily* published multiple editorial articles to stabilize the stock market and decrease the level of chaos in 2015, there were no enthusiastic echoes from the market and from investors (Li, 2015).

This phenomenon is a signal that the official expert system and its dominant position in risk definition in finance have faced huge challenges. I argue that one of the crucial reasons behind this phenomenon is investors' *communication empowerment* (Qiu & Chan, 2011) through digital technologies. For some researchers, one of the crucial promises of digital media to Chinese society is opening a public sphere for ordinary people to engage in politics and public decision-making, as well as to express their own opinions that are possible alternatives to those of dominant actors and institutions (Hu, 2013; Tong & Zuo, 2014). But most of the previous communication studies focused on large-scale social protests that were aroused or supported by cyberspace, and they neglected the more unapparent communication empowerment of digital media in financial markets. What we can observe is that small Chinese investors, alongside official experts, use digital technologies and products, such as easy-to-use stock investing software, online chat rooms and social networking sites, to actively engage in analyzing financial risk. They make the final decisions to buy or sell stocks through ICT at hand, instead of allowing the fund managers to do so. Despite the government's control of the expert system through the licensing of stock analysts, small Chinese investors use their own criteria to evaluate the stock commentator, economist, or financial policy maker online. They also build personal relations with different information sources through digital platforms in an attempt to make sense of big bankers' movements and stock price changes.

Using digital media, these investors revive the social meanings of calculated financial risk and express their concerns about social corruption and inequalities. Since the Chinese stock market officially opened in the 1990s, investors have not raised an Occupy Wall Street-like social protest against inequality in finance. But if we take a close look at what has happened in China's stock market, we can see that individual investors have successfully challenged political regime and capital monopolies in specific crises by using digital technologies and pushing for changes in laws and institutions. In the Everbright "fat-finger error" crash in 2013, for example, while the SSE tried to stabilize the market by declaring that the market was acting normally, numerous investors continued to pressure the SSE on microblog. Along with financial journalists, investors persuaded officials to reveal what truly happened only hours after the SSE's initial claim on market normality and the punishment of Everbright Company afterward (Li, 2014). A more recent case is the 2016 Circuit Breaker crisis. A new government policy caused market panic, and investors expressed their fury online and persuaded the government to suspend the policy and eventually remove Xiao Gang as the head of the China Securities Regulatory Commission (Ying & Soo, 2016).[8]

Another interesting phenomenon is that the big bankers, who are regarded as market manipulators and who gain a fortune at the expense of small investors, also expressed their insecurities with the risk. In some cases, they even actively participated in some digital forms of online protests with small investors. This phenomenon does not mean that the inequalities among the main actors in the financial market, e.g. big bankers, small investors, and the government, have been eliminated in the digital era. Investors still suffer from the chaos of the market. However, the impact of digital technologies on risk definition has resulted in more complicated forms of social inequalities rather than in the binaries of impressing/impressed and exploiting/exploited. Such an impact requires a shift in research focus from media ownership or fixed class categories to more unsystematic and noninstitutional norms and beliefs regarding risk, or, in other words, the *risk cultures* that have been constructed by different actors' communication practices within the risk communities. To achieve such a goal, I have conducted studies in China for more than three years, including on-site observations of ten stock exchange halls and in-depth interviews with fund managers, stock commentators, individual big investors, government officials, media experts, and numerous individual investors. I followed investors to their homes and workplaces to observe how they communicated risk and interacted with other actors. I also used case studies to explore patterns of relevant new media events and determine how these cultural risk communities express their insecurities through digital devices.

In 1998, Hertz published a book named *The Trading Crowd: An Ethnography of the Shanghai Stock Market*, portraying the big picture of China's financial world in its early stages. Twenty years later, it seems that the financial world in Hertz's book has changed to a remarkable degree—not only in its size but also in its form. ICTs have revolutionized the means of communication for Chinese society. For example, Hertz described the financial communication at that time as follows:

> In 1992, all investors, large and dispersed, could avail themselves of what we in the West would consider normal sources of information on the stock market. Indeed, an avalanche of information crashed down around them. The single most important of these sources, for

all Shanghai investors, was the official Shanghai Securities Weekly (Shanghai Zhengquan) published by the Shanghai Securities Exchange. This weekly newspaper contained tables of high, low and closing prices for all stocks and bonds on the market, published explanations and editorials about new regulatory policy, was the official locus for announcements of new share and bond offerings, and ran "society" pieces in which the 'psychology' (xinli) of 'stock people' (gumin) was discussed and analyzed.

(p. 154)

Ms. Lin, the small investor in her fifties, used to buy Shanghai Securities and other financial newspapers on a daily basis in the 1990s, just as Hertz mentioned. However, she vividly pointed out that she does not do so anymore, pulling out her smartphone and saying, "Look, here is the list of official accounts in relation to financial investments that I follow on WeChat."[9] She scrolled down the list: "China Securities, Shanghai Stock Exchange, Shenzhen Stock Exchange, and CSRC ... I have everything here. Stock quotes, instant and free through APP. Stock comments on the official website, free. Why bother buying a newspaper?" Ms. Lin was not alone among the interviewees, a finding consistent with media research regarding the decline of printed media circulation. Decreased newspaper readership is not a new phenomenon in the United States or Europe, but it is truly new to Chinese society in the most recent decade. Put another way, the digital age of China—and the decline of its traditional media—is just beginning. For example, the total retail sales of newspapers across the nation decreased 30% from 2013 to 2014; tellingly, the financial newspapers suffered greatly among all media outlets, a reflection of the impacts of new media outlets. These competitors seem to be delivering financial information in a better way.[10] It's time to revisit the topic that Hertz brought to the table, particularly given the fact that these new phenomena may be affecting the power dynamics and social atmosphere of China's financial world. As a communications scholar, instead of drawing a full map of China's stock markets like Hertz, I instead put financial communication and the communicative construction of risk cultures at the center of this discussion. Indeed, these topics form the very essence of this book, examining the role that digital media play.

Stock markets have promises to human societies, and so do digital media. A stock market, in theory, should ensure that good firms obtain the money they need to expand and promote themselves, and second, to reward investors with the fruits of these companies' development. Ideally, such a market would create a win-win relation for the whole society. The digital media, as celebrated by many scholars, would change social dynamics by granting the silenced ones and minor groups a space for actions. Why these promises are sometimes fulfilled and other times unfulfilled? What are the consequences, with regard to current risk societies, when stock markets meet digital media? This book endeavors to provide some answers to these questions from a communication researcher's perspective.

Chapter Summaries

To understand how financial risk is staged and communicated in order to eventually form a risk culture of consensus, we have to examine the stage itself, along with its major characters. In this book, traditional and digital media together form the stage, and the communicators of the financial world act as the major players on it. Chapter 2 sets the media stage of China at large and the one of financial communication in particular. It reveals the complicated power dynamics of this arena under the larger backdrop of marketization in an authoritarian country. In the digital media era, the government still holds tight control of the mass communication system through ownership. At the same time, the emergence of privately owned social media outlets has granted the public, especially grassroots movements, an influential social place to voice their own opinions. These groups' power remains somewhat limited because the political regime gradually has applied more skilled and strong-armed censorship mechanisms.

The particular media stage of financial communication is no exception to the general rule of China's media systems, but it does present some very unique characteristics. From the media's end, competition among financial media has stimulated them to invite the participation of popular risk definers, a phenomenon that has resulted in the rise of a nongovernment expert system. In response, the government has created a license system in order to exert control over who can be considered an expert communicator. Distrusting this licensed expert system, investors started to not only communicate financial issues themselves but also to evaluate and select their own experts online, some of whom are unlicensed. Because the level of cyber censorship and self-censorship is comparatively low when it comes to financial issues, digital media indeed is changing the power dynamics of financial communication, creating a social space alternative to the government-owned and government-licensed expert system.

After providing a rough overview of the media stage of financial risk and its main characters/communicators, the book then turns to the specific communication practices of big and small investors. These two groups interpret different types of economic or financial information in divergent ways, and their communicative interactions with other characters represent a diverse and complicated tapestry. Thus, Chapters 3–6 emphasize communication (especially from the investors' end), as conducted for each type of financial information; this discussion includes the power dynamics created and confronted during such communication processes. Chapter 3 starts with "very basic information" in the eyes of today's Chinese investors, namely stock quotes and trading orders. In the 1990s, ICTs were gradually gaining ground in China with limited and centralized usage. Through the efforts of the financial system's initial designers, transactions were digitalized at the very beginning of the stock markets. This feature made communication of stock quotes and trading orders smoother and faster than the majority of global stock markets in their early days. These communication advantages, however, only benefited the very few. Without ICTs, basic information like stock prices—the starting point of the entire investment process—was once "owned" by big investors with PC software devices and Internet access provided by brokerage firms. They also enjoyed privileges in sending out and accessing their trading orders. The small investors had to stay in the big stock exchange hall, sharing a computer or electronic screen for limited information. Then, they had to wait in a long queue to fulfill their orders. The inequality of ICT ownership resulted in a power hierarchy of financial communication, with small investors totally excluded from the risk definer position, because they lacked even the most basic market information. Later, the widespread distribution of personal computers and then smartphones broke down existing power dynamics. Suddenly, all investors could enjoy instant and detailed information related to stock quotes. Small investors could send out their trading orders instantly, just like the big investors.

Since big and small investors now begin at the same starting line with regard to financial communication, the question becomes one of who interprets basic information better. The answer should determine the dominant risk position in the financial world. Under such circumstances, it seems to be a *non sequitur* that an expert-oriented risk culture would dominate the markets, because experts are supposed to do a better job of transforming the uncertainties of stock quotes into possibilities. Chapter 4, however, explains why experts have not gained the upper hand by analyzing the communication of national- and international-level information, which includes national affairs (national policies and state economic reports) and international news. The mediation of national affairs through state-controlled mass and new media should reinforce the government's risk definer position in deciding the direction of national economics at large and financial markets in particular. However, the counter-discourse that challenges the official one is always there, and it is becoming louder and louder in the digital media age. This phenomenon is prompting the government to take action to win back public trust. Positive or negative, the financial world has reached a consensus that national affairs greatly impact China's stock markets; compared with these internal affairs, international news fails to influence financial markets to the same degree. Therefore, the investors, especially the nonprofessional ones, lack the desire to learn about global affairs and the opinions of international finance companies. They may consider such information for reference, with ICT delivering this global information quickly and easily. That being said, China's financial markets are becoming more and more open to the world, and this situation could change in the future.

All in all, the predominantly strong policy maker and closed-door conditions invalidate the professional analyses of financial markets; meanwhile, the economic conditions have been separated from the market performance. Together, they have resulted in the dismantling of Western professionalism in China's financial world, preventing the rise of a dominant expert culture. Chapter 5 discusses how the experts then put up a second fight in interpreting company information, which includes randomly released company news and regularly released financial statements. In the ICT era, all investors seem to be standing at the same starting line again; in theory, all of the digital media users can receive company information at the same time. What matters should be the professional interpretation of the information and the evaluation of a listed company's future conditions. However, the high level of social corruption and comparatively low level of law enforcement have resulted in a public distrust of the information generated or released by accounting firms, law firms, listed companies, and mass media. Unable to seize the dominant position in financial communication through professionalism, the big investors have turned to using their advantaged position in capital as a weapon, building up gray, if not illegal, guanxi with the listed companies and media makers. This way, they can manipulate the markets and even "polish" the company information themselves to ensure their own security at the expense of small investors. These questionable tactics eventually caused a separation between the company's performance and its stock performance, devaluing the publicly communicated company information.

Small investors, on the other hand, respond to the risk situation by picking their own "experts" online, experts that they believe have the specific "expertise" to deal with financial risk in China. Such expertise does not necessitate hardcore financial knowledge or theories, but a specific understanding of China's policies, the ability to predict the moves of big bankers, and/or the resources to know a company's insider information. The small investors have turned their attention to the communication of stock commentaries, a topic discussed in Chapter 6. The communicators of stock commentary are called stock commentators in China. In finance, the public figures of stock commentators usually represent the "facework"[11] of the expert system's hidden transactions in the financial world. In the 1990s, before ICTs began to flourish, the small investors supported and even elected their own experts by gathering around these persons physically, listening to their public talks about market predictions and stock analysis. The mass media found an opportunity in the market demand of such facework, inviting the popular commentators to publish their opinions through various media outlets. The government, on the other hand, saw the uncertainties related to these rising stars in the nongovernment expert system. As the 1990s finished up, they seized back the power of financial communication by enforcing a license system for stock commentators. Only individuals who receive government approval can legally communicate their commentary as stock commentators through the mass media. The once scattered and nongovernment experts became institutionalized, usually representing a fund or brokerage. The small investors could not evaluate and decide on their experts; rather, the government, local finance companies, and media outlets did the job for them. However, social corruption among the stock commentators, as well as media and self-censorship issues tended to prevent frank stock analysis. Meanwhile, the criteria of the license system were not adept at selecting the best experts for the public. As such, the small investors refused to blindly follow this new expert system. Instead, they turned to digital media platforms, not only using their comments to evaluate the licensed commentators on mass media but also selecting the unlicensed commentators that they found more capable. These unlicensed stock commentators lure small investors into participating in member-only private channels online, gaining membership and even spreading false information to their "customers" to manipulate the market. As small investors fight for their own territory in evaluating risk definers through digital media, new risk simultaneously emerges.

In sum, this book reviews the full map of financial communication in China, explaining the reasons that the expert-oriented risk culture— whether government-led or government-licensed expert led—has failed to flourish. It further elucidates on the role of ICTs in these troubled waters. The investors' distrust toward the expert system is based upon their understanding of the status quo, rather than the result of irrationality or greediness. They are aware of the fact that traditional professionalism has been dismantled in China's financial world, particularly in terms of the absolute dominance of the political regime over economics, the corruption existing in various social dimensions, and the comparative isolation of the local market within the global system. The information being publicly communicated is untrustworthy and devalued, making the economic conditions of any industry or security nearly unreadable. Under such circumstances, the big investors have used their capital instead of expertise as an advantage, developing illegal *guanxi* to manipulate the securities at the expense of small investors and the stability of the market as a whole. The small investor, on the other hand, has protested online fiercely against this problematic system, refusing to blindly follow the risk definers who they believe are corrupt and dishonest. With ICT as weapon, they seized autonomy in financial investment and took on the position of evaluating the experts, attempting to ascertain alternative ways to interpret the market conditions. Ironically, their efforts have resulted in the rise of an unlicensed expert system, one that lures them into developing *guanxi* relations through online memberships, manipulating them by communicating often fake analysis or insider information. At the end of this book, I discuss two notable phenomena that may influence the future struggles between the expert- and guanxi-oriented risk cultures in China. One is the deepening of the globalization process in China's financial markets, a process that may result in the rise of global finance companies as important risk definers and financial communicators. Another important aspect that should not be overlooked is the government's attitude. What strategies will the government choose to use in order to promote its own expert system? How will it deal with cyberspace discussions? The answers to these questions will have drastic impacts on the future power dynamics of financial communication in China.

Notes

1 In China's stock market, red numbers indicate that share prices have risen, while green ones mean the prices have gone down.
2 Sanhu can also be translated as "scattered accounts" (Keith et al., 2014) or "dispersed players" (Hertz, 1998) in English. In this book, I use the term "small investors" to highlight wealth as the major difference between them and the big investors.
3 Big banker (*zhuangjia*) is the nickname for big investors in China. Here, "banker" refers to one participating in the gambling games.
4 The people's sayings and doings were derived from the recorded data or directly observed by the research participants.
5 In Chinese, *guanxi* means interpersonal relations. It may imply rent seeking and other corruptive activities (see Tsui & Farh, 1997; Farh et al., 1998; Tsang, 1998).
6 Read the full post on Spotify's website: https://newsroom.spotify.com/2018-04-02/tomorrow/
7 This case will be discussed in Chapter 6.
8 I will talk about the Circuit Breaker Crisis in detail in Chapter 4 of this book.
9 First launched in 2011, WeChat is the dominant digital platform in China. It mainly provides communication services like social media. The platform defines its "official account service" as follows:

> The WeChat Official Account Admin Platform is a cooperation and promotion service launched for famous persons, government, media, and enterprises. Official accounts can promote their brands to billions of WeChat users through this WeChat channel, thus reducing propagation costs, raising brand popularity, and building up more influential brand images.
>
> (See https://admin.wechat.com/cgi-bin/readtemplate?
> t=ibg_en/en_faq_tmpl)

Some researchers have examined WeChat and its official account services in detail (Lien & Cao, 2014; Chan, 2015; Xu et al., 2015).

10 This data was retrieved from www.cssn.cn/xwcbx/xwcbx_cmjj/201507/ t20150722_2089505.shtml
11 The original idea of "facework" and the hidden transaction system comes from the Society for the Advancement of Socio-Economics. It was presented at a mini-conference entitled "Global Finance: Hidden and Public Dimensions" organized by Karin Knorr-Cetina and Alexandra Preda. See the introduction of the conference here: https://sase.org/event/2018-kyoto/#mini

References

Abolafia, M. (2001). *Making markets: Opportunism and restraint on Wall Street*. Cambridge, MA: Harvard University Press.

Adam, B., & van Loon, J. (2000). Introduction: Repositioning risk: The challenge for social theory. In B. Adam, U. Beck, & J. van Loon (Eds.) *The risk society and beyond: Critical issues for social theory* (pp. 1–32). London: SAGE Publications Ltd.

Beck, U. (1992). *Risk society: Towards a new modernity*. London: Sage.

Beck, U. (2006). Living in the world risk society: A Hobhouse Memorial Public Lecture given on Wednesday 15 February 2006 at the London School of Economics. *Economy and Society*, 35(3), 329–345.

Beck U. (2009). *World at risk*. Cambridge: Polity Press.

Bell, M. M., & Mayerfeld, D. B. (1999). The rationalization of risk. Society and Natural Resources, Draft of March, 25.

Couldry, N. (2004). Theorising media as practice. *Social Semiotics*, 14(2), 115–132.

Craig, R. T. (2006). Communication as a practice. In G. J. Shepherd, J. St. John, & T. Striphas (Eds.) *Communication as ...: Perspectives on theory* (pp. 38–47). Thousand Oaks, CA: Sage.

Chung, C. Y., Lee, J., & Park, J. (2014). Are individual investors uninformed? Evidence from trading behaviors by heterogeneous investors around unfaithful corporate disclosure. *Asia-Pacific Journal of Financial Studies*, 43(2), 157–182.

De Bondt, W. F. (1998). A portrait of the individual investor. *European economic review*, 42(3–5), 831–844.

DeLong, J. B., Shleifer, A., Summers, L. H., & Waldmann, R. J. (1987). The economic consequences of noise traders. National Bureau of Economic Research, NBER Working Paper Series, 2395.

Dimson, E., Marsh, P., & Staunton, M. (2003) Global evidence on the equity risk premium. *Journal of Applied Corporate Finance*, 15(4), 27–38.

Dominick, J. R. (2010). *The dynamics of mass communication: Media in the digital age*. New York: Tata McGraw-Hill Education.

Du, J. (2007). The media analysis of the blogger's fraud case. *Journalists*, 9, 24–27.

Farh, J. L., Tsui, A. S., Xin, K., & Cheng, B. S. (1998). The influence of relational demography and guanxi: The Chinese case. *Organization Science*, 9(4), 471–488.

Foster, S. (1998). Justice from the ground up: Distributive inequities, grassroots resistance, and the transformative politics of the environmental justice movement. *California Law Review*, 86, 775.

Freudenberg, N., & Steinsapir, C. (1991). Not in our backyards: The grassroots environmental movement. *Society & Natural Resources, 4*(3), 235–245.

Frickel, S. (2004). Just science? Organizing scientist activism in the US environmental justice movement. *Science as Culture, 13*(4), 449–469.

Frickel, S. (2011). Who are the experts of environmental health justice. In G. Ottinger & B. R. Cohen (Eds.) *Technoscience and environmental justice: Expert cultures in a grassroots movement* (pp. 21–39). Cambridge, MA: MIT Press.

Gaby, S., & Caren, N. (2012). Occupy online: How cute old men and Malcolm X recruited 400,000 US users to OWS on Facebook. *Social Movement Studies, 11*(3–4), 367–374.

Gamble, J. E. (1997). Stir-fried stocks: Share dealers, trading places, and new options in contemporary Shanghai. *Modern China, 23*(2), 181–215.

Giddens, A. (1984). *The constitution of society*. Cambridge: Polity.

Giddens, A. (1991). *Modernity and self-identity*. Cambridge: Polity.

Giddens, A. (1994). Living in a post-traditional society. In U. Beck, A. Giddens, & S. Lash (Eds.) *Reflexive modernization* (pp. 56–109). Cambridge: Polity.

Giddens, A. (2013*). The consequences of modernity*. Stanford, CA: Stanford University Press.

Green, S. (2003). *China's stockmarket: A guide to its progress, players and prospects*. London: Economist Books in association with Profile Books Ltd.

Harris, L. (1998). Circuit breakers and program trading limits: What have we learned. *Brookings-Wharton Papers on Financial Services, 63*.

Hertz, E. (1998). *The trading crowd: An ethnography of the Shanghai stock market* (Vol. 108). Cambridge: Cambridge University Press.

Hu, Y. (2013). The Internet and social mobilization in China. *Frontiers in New Media Research, 15*, 93.

Humphreys, P. (1996). Mass media and media policy in Western Europe (Vol. 2). Manchester: Manchester University Press.

Japanese Statistics Bureau (2017) Official data of Japanese stock market. Retrieved from https://www.stat.go.jp/english/

Johnson, J. R., & Ranco, D. J. (2011). Risk assessment and Native Americans at the cultural crossroads: Making better science or redefining health? In G. Ottinger & B. R. Cohen (Eds.) *Technoscience and environmental justice: Expert cultures in a grassroots movement* (pp. 179–199). Cambridge, MA: MIT Press.

Kaiser, J. (2000). Ecologists on a mission to save the world. *Science, 287*(5456), 1188–1192.

Kang, J., Liu, M. H., & Ni, S. X. (2002). Contrarian and momentum strategies in the China stock market: 1993–2000. *Pacific-Basin Finance Journal, 10*(3), 243–265.

Keith, M., Lash, S., Arnoldi, J., & Rooker, T. (2014). *China constructing capitalism*. London: Routledge.

Kupiec, P. H. (1996). Noise traders, excess volatility, and a securities transactions tax. *Journal of Financial Services Research, 10*(2), 115–129.

Lash, S. (2000). Risk culture. In B. Adam, U. Beck, & J. Van Loon (Eds.) *The risk society and beyond: Critical issues for social theory* (pp. 47–72). London: Sage.

Li, H. (2014). The asserting of the insider trading in the fat finger event of Everbright securities. *Journal of Heilongjiang Administrative Cadre College of Politics and Law, 1*, 28.

Li, S. (2015). Analysis of people's daily's report of saving the stock market during the financial crashes. *Journal of News Research*, 15, 264.

Lien, C. H., & Cao, Y. (2014). Examining WeChat users' motivations, trust, attitudes, and positive word-of-mouth: Evidence from China. *Computers in Human Behavior*, 41, 104–111.

Mazur, A. (1998). Global environmental change in the news: 1987–90 vs 1992–6. *International Sociology*, 13(4), 457–472.

McCormick, S. (2007). Democratizing science movements: A new framework for mobilization and contestation. *Social Studies of Science*, 37(4), 609–623.

McQuail, D. (1994). *Mass communication*. London and Thousand Oaks, CA: New Delhi SAGE.

Ng, L., & Wu, F. (2010). Peer effects in the trading decisions of individual investors. *Financial Management*, 39(2), 807–831.

Nieusma, D. (2011). Middle-out social change: Expert-led development interventions in Sri Lanka's energy sector. In G. Ottinger & B. R. Cohen (Eds.) *Technoscience and environmental justice: Expert cultures in a grassroots movement, Urban and industrial environments* (pp. 119–146). Cambridge, MA: MIT Press.

Pauwels, M. (2015). Occupy Wall Street—anything more than a fly in the ointment? In L. Cossu-Beaumont, J. H., Coste, & J. B. Velut (Eds.) *The crisis and renewal of US capitalism: A civilizational approach to modern American political economy* (pp. 551–562). London: Routledge.

Qiu, L., & Chan, T. (2011). *Studies of new media events*. Beijing: People's University Press.

Rome, A. (2003). "Give earth a chance": The environmental movement and the sixties. *The Journal of American History*, 90(2), 525–554.

Schatzki, T. R. (2010). *Site of the social: A philosophical account of the constitution of social life and change*. University Park: Pennsylvania State University Press.

Schiller, D. (2000). *Digital capitalism*. Cambridge, MA: MIT Press.

Sparks, C., & Reading, A. (1997). *Communism, capitalism and the mass media*. London: Sage.

Tong, J., & Zuo, L. (2014). Weibo communication and government legitimacy in China: A computer-assisted analysis of Weibo messages on two "mass incidents". *Information, Communication & Society*, 17(1), 66–85.

Tsang, E. W. (1998). Can guanxi be a source of sustained competitive advantage for doing business in China? *The Academy of Management Executive*, 12(2), 64–73.

Tsui, A. S., & Farh, J. L. L. (1997). Where guanxi matters: Relational demography and guanxi in the Chinese context. *Work and Occupations*, 24(1), 56–79.

Xu, J., Kang, Q., Song, Z., & Clarke, C. P. (2015). Applications of mobile social media: WeChat among academic libraries in China. *The Journal of Academic Librarianship*, 41(1), 21–30.

Yang, G., & Calhoun, C. (2007). Media, civil society, and the rise of a green public sphere in China. *China Information*, 21(2), 211–236.

Ying, T. & Soo, A. (2016, February 20). China removes Xiao as CSRC head after stock market meltdown. Retrieved from http://www.bloomberg.com/news/articles/2016-02-19/head-of-china-s-securities-regulator-to-step-down-wsj-reports

2 Major Players of Risk Communication

Many people consider the financial markets in China to be mythical. Some regard them as a playground for gold prospectors. Still others view them as dangerous gambling houses run by socialist strangers. These mixed feelings about China's young markets can be summed up with these major questions: How do the capitalist markets interact with the powerful government? Is Big Brother in charge or do big capitalists take the lead? Why is there so much excessive speculation in China? Under these circumstances, who wins and who loses? Have the stock markets made China's society more equal, or have they widened the gap between the rich and the poor? Are small investors simply pawns to the big bankers?

Researchers provide very different answers to the above questions, depending on how they approach the topic. As mentioned in Chapter 1, this book tries to answer these questions from the perspective of risk communication. The readers may imagine the existence of a community that faces financial crashes and surges together. Within this community, financial risk, or uncertainty in finance, is staged, understood, and communicated daily by the community's members, using shared languages and concepts collectively, but not equally. I will focus on the interactions of six of the members, including the government, the companies, the journalists, the stock commentators, the small investors, and the big "bankers". They perform the roles of different characters—or, in other words, *risk positions* (Beck, 1992)—on this stage. Some are governors of risk, and some are disciplined; some win big, and some lose their fortunes to crashes. Some are active talkers and help define risk; others are passive listeners following others. These various characters, or the members of financial community, do not always agree upon their roles set up by the people in authorities. When we take a close look at the interactions among the members, we can view constant struggles and challenges when communicating financial issues. Those who take an upper hand politically or capitally have struggled to maintain their dominant risk positions, while the underdogs do not want to give it up without a fight. The intensity of such controversies is so high, to the extent that it has changed the melodrama of risk communication in finance, regardless of the original scripts set up by the dominant expert system.

But what exactly influences the characters' actions and interactions during the communications process? If, for example, the stage settings left no room for confrontations and challenges from the bottom up, or if they simply excluded minor groups from the stage in the first place, it would be game changing for the financial world of China. Thus, before we examine different characters who stage risk through their communications, this chapter starts with the stage itself—the media system in China.

Mass Media, New Media, and Financial Media in China

Media have always been a formidable propaganda machine for the Chinese Communist Party. After coming to power, the party soon legitimized their underground radio stations and unlicensed newspapers while nationalizing and centralizing media outlets in the private sector (Sukosd & Wang, 2013). More powerful than ever, the party's mass communication efficiency reached its peak during the Cultural Revolution period from 1966 to 1976. During this time, the Chinese media simply served as a mouthpiece of the government, delivering its policies and promoting socialist ideologies (Lu, 2004). When China opened its doors to the capitalist world after 1978, however, the ideological state apparatus (ISA) (Althusser, 2006) suddenly found itself still owned by the state yet self-financing, struggling to satisfy market needs while remaining completely loyal to the government (Latham, 2000). The media managers eventually worked out strategies to survive in this new situation. Putting aside national politics, it became clear that people cared about and were interested in other social issues. The national- and province-level news agencies then started to establish subsidiary-like newspapers, magazines, and TV channels (later with websites and online platforms). These subsidiaries commonly embrace lighter media content like entertainment, sports, finance, and international news. These features appear alongside reports on national politics (e.g. Hong, 1998a; Bai, 2005; Liu & McCormick, 2011). Using this strategy, newspaper managers commonly keep the party newspaper while launching a so-called "metropolis newspaper" (Chen, 2007; Han, 2011) to lure customers with city lifestyles. Ultimately, these publications get more advertisers compared to the party newspapers due to their "metropolis" style. Readers can catch up with the latest government affairs on the front page before moving on to explore current affairs locally and globally. Whereas the party newspapers continue to serve the interests of the government (earning fewer subscribers nowadays), the metropolis newspapers have become the profit-makers sustaining the "mother company" (Hong, 1998b; Zhao, 1998). Observers may notice the same strategies being applied by magazines, radio channels, and TV stations. To smoothen such marketization, the Chinese government has permitted the establishment of media groups through an official department that has a certain degree of autonomy in human resources and management, thus better managing market needs (Lee, He, & Huang, 2007). But regarding administrative levels, the party media has greater power than the entertainment media, thus keeping the entire media system in its orbit.

The media managers also observe the special needs of their customers who require in-depth and detailed information regarding a particular social aspect, therefore not concentrating on a variety of issues. Such needs indeed come from China's economic reform at large—sports have become a business instead of merely a national honor, women have started to wear makeup and dresses, and investors are eager to test the waters in the financial markets. To satisfy these customers, there has been a renaissance of sports newspapers, fashion magazines, and financial media outlets—from TV programs, radio channels, newspaper outlets, to economic magazines and eventually online platform. When finance has garnered its own publications in this new media environment, various popular media outlets compete for market share. Some popular examples include, but are not limited to, the television channel CCTV-2, the media group China Business Network, the financial newspaper *China Securities Journal*, and the financial magazine *Caijing*. These media channels and platforms provide a prototype when examining the different communicators of financial risk.

The flourishing of these finance-specific media outlets is nothing new for societies in possession of active financial markets. Nor is it particularly surprising in the context of an emerging economy. As Chakravartty and Schiller (2010) noted, there exists an interesting phenomenon in which developing economies with more immature markets tend to demonstrate more eagerness in building up financial media compared to developed countries. What is unique about China's situation can be found in the ownership of these nascent media outlets. From a political economist's point of view, the government once exerted complete control over financial risk in its earliest forms. Indeed, as of this book's writing (and into the foreseeable future), most of China's TV stations, radio channels, newspapers, and magazines remain under the state's control, aside from a few notable exceptions.[1] Media with economic- and finance-oriented content are no exception. For example, CCTV-2 belongs to China Central Television, the predominant state TV broadcaster in China.[2] Belonging to Shanghai Media Group, a state-owned company, China Business Network owns an influential newspaper, TV channel, financial magazine, and web portal.[3] *China Securities Journal* was launched by Xinhua News Agency, the influential state press news agency.[4] The magazine *Caijing* is owned by SEEC Media Group Limited, a group controlled by United Home Limited, a half-government institution that technically designed and established the mechanical systems of the Shanghai and Shenzhen Stock Markets (Ma, 2003). Since 2015, *Caijing* and SEEC Group have been part of the China International Trust Investment Corporation, or the CITIC Group, a state-owned finance company of China.

It appears that we can always trace financial media outlets back to state ownership, but attention should be paid to the internal differences between them. Some province- or city-level media, for example, are more liberal and open compared to the conservative and centralized national media (Qiang, 2004; Gang & Bandurski, 2011). Moreover, facing marketization, these financial media inevitably compete with each other for large audiences; as a result, they have to work out ways to surpass their peers in terms of their style of reporting, focus, content, and experts—from editors, journalists, and program hosts to their columnists and guest speakers. Such choices inevitably produce diversification, causing some financial media publications, like *Caijing* magazine, to stand out as more radical than others, eagerly reporting on sensitive issues, including market corruption and manipulation (Cheng, 2008; Guo, Chan, & Huang, 2017).

Given that some of these financial media outlets enjoy a certain level of autonomy, the problem remains as to what extent they can exercise it. Apparently, they have little wiggle room when it comes to certain types of financial information, like *national affairs*.[5] When communicating information from the policy makers, they must serve as the government's mouthpiece, correctly and swiftly reporting on economic conditions or official policies. Suspicious and negative comments are allowed in terms of technical issues, but they must be made very cautiously. In terms of other information, not directly related to the government like *company information* and *stock quotes*, the state-owned mass media can navigate more freely with a larger range of motion. Media actors can make analyses, predictions, or critiques. Professional communicators are eager to demonstrate their competence on these issues in order to become known as strong risk definers, surpassing others in the media. To win the audience's favor, it is not uncommon to see the media fiercely point a finger at a corrupt company or a problematic fund, but it would be almost earth-shattering if they were to do so with policy makers.

If it's ownership that predominantly matters in the power games of financial communication, it seems that the popularity of new media/social media in China may completely change the financial communication stage. Of course, upon entering the digital age, these state-owned media began applying a multi-platform strategy, developing their own online platforms including web portals, news apps, and social media accounts. These pieces should be regarded as mere extensions of the former outlets: One should not expect any fundamental differences between the main publication and its sub-platforms. For instance, the content, tone, ideology, and even comments remain extremely consistent among the People's Daily; its web portal online, also called the People's Daily; the sub-forum Qiangguo BBS; and its microblog, blog sites, and official accounts on third-party social media (e.g. Parsons & Xu, 2001; Hung, 2003; Li, Xuan, & Kluver, 2003; Li & Long, 2017). Communication researchers have devoted a great deal of attention to privately owned new media, where indeed the change in power dynamics has been most apparent. Privately operated blogs, forums, chat rooms, microblogs, smartphone apps, and various communication platforms have provided Chinese individuals and minor groups an inexpensive channel for delivering their opinions to the public. A milestone case can be seen in the mediation of the Sun Zhigang incident. In 2003, a 27-year-old man was found dead after enduring physical abuse at a detention center in Guangzhou.[6] He initially was detained for not carrying his ID card or a so-called temporary living permit, a permit that one must apply for if he or she is not a local resident of a province/city.[7] The local police detained Sun due to China's custody and repatriation system based on a government regulation begun in 1982. Three days after he was taken into custody, his family was notified of his death. People were furious when Sun's tragedy was reported by the province-level media (as discussed above, more liberal than central news). Influential opinion leaders took to their blogs while ordinary netizens reached out on BBS and in chat rooms to protest online, ultimately seeking justice for Sun (Yu, 2006; Hassid, 2012). Facing this cyberspace demonstration, the government responded to the public in a surprisingly positive way. Not only did officials urge a police investigation of Sun's case, which eventually sent multiple individuals to prison, but they also reconsidered the legal basis of the custody and repatriation system. In June 2003, only about two months after these Internet activities, the government announced that the system would be abolished the following August (Zhu, 2006).

Sun's case is incredibly important in understanding the Chinese context because it demonstrates that collective actions on the Internet can not only create collective memories—which not many researchers would argue against—but that these protests can persuade political and institutional changes in an authoritarian society. From that moment on, researchers have started to use sociologist Habermas's (1989, 1996, 2001) concept of the *public sphere* to describe China's cyberspace. Such researchers have asserted that the new media will create a social space for the grassroots to express their opinions, thereby stimulating social and political reform toward liberalism (e.g. Zheng & Wu, 2005; Wu, 2007; Gang & Bandurski, 2011). Indeed, equipped with new media platforms, Chinese netizens have not been shy about joining movements at the national, institutional, or personal level, demanding civil rights and protesting against corruption and injustice (Qiu & Chan, 2009). To date, they have successfully persuaded the government to punish multiple polluting companies and remove corrupt officials. They also have helped minority groups though online charities. Taking a closer look at these collective actions online, we find that the majority bursts out at a critical or crisis moment, when the level of uncertainty or risk surrounding a certain issue is sky-high. People view the issue with a keen eye: Is the company, for example, pouring poisoned water into our rivers? Is nuclear energy safe enough for us to allow such a power plant into our community? Is the government official guilty just because he is wearing a watch that apparently exceeds his budget? In the mass media era of yesteryear, when these questions came about, it was the government-oriented risk definers who stood up to clarify the situation for the public—if the questions were even asked in the first place.

On this new stage of risk, previously marginalized characters and audiences have begun to play a larger role. In the field of environmental protection, for instance, a bottom-up green movement has emerged that shares many parallels to those in Europe and the United States, except for the fact that it primarily has roots in cyberspace, as mentioned in Chapter 1. Researchers have used the term *green public sphere* to describe the collective environmental protections of these netizens (Yang, 2006; Yang & Calhoun, 2007; Sima, 2011), celebrating the rise of civil society in the Chinese context.

Other researchers, however, remain less optimistic about the new media revolution in China, regardless of its private ownership. The reason is simple. These researchers believe that the seemingly active communication in the digital realm exists simply because it caught the government off-guard. Official authorities were unfamiliar with the Internet and its netizens. After an initial phase of observation and analysis, the officials began to supervise cyberspace more skillfully, adopting real-name registration for web portals and social media accounts. They have established discourse guide mechanisms and algorithms for the censorship system (see Herold, 2008; Wallis, 2011; Lagerkvist, 2012; Fu, Chan, & Chau, 2013; Yang, 2013). The privately owned new media platforms are willing to cooperate with the government as well, conducting self-censorship work (MacKinnon, 2011; King, Pan, & Roberts, 2013). They self-censor, sometimes even before the political regime steps in, in exchange for official support and licenses. It seems that the government once again has become a main character on the new media stage, keeping the cyberspace players at bay.

Clashes between the new liberalism and government authorities have resulted in a controversial form of media communication in China. On the one hand, we are witnessing the empowerment of the once silent masses, and on the other hand, we are seeing the rise of "networked authoritarianism" (MacKinnon, 2011). But what about the field of finance specifically? Generally speaking, the level of cyber censorship in finance is indeed very low. This fact may come as a surprise to some researchers—especially those focused on censorship issues in China. However, the government demonstrates a generally tolerant attitude toward the media stage of this important social sector. Radical critics can be found nearly everywhere online, including finance-specific and general social media platforms, forums, web portal comments, and chat rooms. Their wrath may be directed at the individuals or institutions at government departments, the banks, the funds, or the listed companies themselves. The netizens are quite free to engage in satire and make jokes about topical issues in finance, without being silenced or punished. This tolerance is extended even during critical junctions, like the Circuit Breaker Crisis, which will be discussed in more detail in the following chapters. Occurring at the beginning of 2016, the crisis spurred furious investors to dominate social media, fiercely blaming the new circuit breaker policy of the China Securities Regulatory Commission (CSRC) for causing market panic. Little of this discourse was censored. It's hard to imagine a similar tolerance being extended in any other social dimension.

Why is this the case? From the government's point of view, finance is a crucial yet not so sensitive issue. To be more specific, financial risk is less likely to shake the political regime, compared to other risks like environmental catastrophes, political corruption, and human rights struggles. The major participants in the financial markets are not necessarily rich, but they are not the weak of the weak among proletariats, the real grassroots movers who form the most fiercely rebellious groups across various societies (e.g. Alexander, 2010; Özerdem & Podder, 2012; Alexander & Pfaffe, 2014). The driving force of these groups comes from rage about their poor living conditions, from their belief that they are abused and exploited by the existing social structure. Compared with these people of low social-economic stature, these investors have something to lose if they have something to invest. This fact undeniably stops them from risking what they already own to protest against the regime. The evidence of this truism can be seen in the fact that since the establishment of the stock markets, only small-scale street protests have occurred, the targets of which have tended to be particular listed companies. Many other investors have chosen to protest their own interests through lawsuits, and it is fairly common for their calls to be responded to or at least partially satisfied by the legal system. As such, the direct tension between the government and investors is relatively low.

Another reason for the government's relaxed stance lies in the unique characteristics of financial risk, namely that the sufferers of stock crises are also the potential benefactors of a bull market. In 2006, for example, the composite indexes of the Shanghai Stock Exchange (SSE) and Shenzhen Stock Exchange (SZSE) climbed to nearly 130% for the year, and the huge surge extended to 2007, creating one of the most famous bull market periods in China's stock history (Arouri, & Liu, 2008; Yao & Luo, 2009). When I mentioned the 2006 bull market to the investors being interviewed, the majority of them said that they enjoyed the fruits of this market soar; a few even doubled or tripled their money.

Because the winners knowingly risk becoming losers, they represent less of a threat than those who suffer from other social ailments. Victims of air pollution or war crimes have every right to protest against the source of their problems, but people may question if investors are in a position to do the same when it comes to market problems. Meanwhile, investors themselves are sometimes blamed as the exact cause of market chaos, communicating rumors and increasing excessive speculation. Thus, there is a lack of social consensus surrounding investors' protests of the injustices inherent to the current financial structure. Some investors believe that they themselves must take full responsibility for their losses in the financial market.

All in all, the government and financial investors seem to have reached an unspoken agreement. On the one hand, public discussion about finance is allowed so long as commentators do not directly attack the ultimate authority of the regime, or at least not in a radical or threatening way. Investors agree upon the good intentions of the policy makers, believing that their regulations and policies seek to stabilize the markets (regardless of the results of these actions). Against this backdrop, investors focus on technical issues most of the time while avoiding direct confrontations against the political regime—even though financial risk is always a combination of technical and political problems. When investors do point a finger at officials, they only go so far as to emphasize a particular department or institution rather than the entire central government. They are careful to criticize their ability rather than their authority. In return, the government shows benevolence toward the critical discourse from the public regarding financial issues, allowing a space for communicators in cyberspace.

From a critical researcher's perspective, it would seem that these tame conditions would fail to stimulate anything revolutionary in the financial world. Indeed, it is clear that the government still controls the financial-content mass media in terms of ownership, just as they control other types of traditional media outlets. Only government-licensed experts can express their opinions about the stock markets in mainstream media. To garner larger audiences, some mass media programs have allowed the small investors to voice their perspectives in the form of scrolling text at the bottom of the screen during TV programs or call-in radio shows. In this context, public involvement overall is very low. The audience and participants are scripted to play the role of questioners or complainers, while the program hosts and guests represent the expert system, answering questions and explaining the system to them. However, the unique relationship between the government and the public on the issue of finance has resulted in a surprising consequence— the "noise," small investors' online presence—is becoming louder and louder, so much so that they are drowning out the experts' voices on mass media. The cyber communicators have no hesitation when commenting on financial policies and evaluating *stock commentary* made by the *stock commentators* or fund managers, a fact that shakes the very base of the government and its licensed expert system. This phenomenon has changed the power dynamics on the media stage of risk. Some unlicensed analysts and commentators who could not appear on government-controlled mass media have started to gain public favor through forum posts, (micro)blogs, and chat rooms. They even have more popularity than many licensed experts. One of the most infamous examples is *daitoudage*,[8] a person who didn't have any educational background in finance. Winning the trust of numerous small investors, he had a blog that received over 30 million clicks by the time he was arrested in 2007 for illegal business (Bian, 2014). His blog was one of the most read blogs in China, surpassing those written by high-exposure celebrities. For more on this topic, see Chapter 6, which examines the communication of *stock commentary* in great detail.

At the end of this section, let's take a final look at the entire map of the media stage of financial risk. Before China's political and economic reforms, there were no financial media outlets—simply because there were no financial markets. With the birth of stock markets in China, the market need for finance-related information increased, persuading many state-owned media and financial intuitions to create outlets and platforms specifically geared at satisfying these investors. Under the big umbrella of the media system in China, the financial mass media joined in the marketization and liberalization reforms, but simultaneously remained under the control of authoritarianism (Chan & Qiu, 2002). Though they continue with their duty to serve as the government's mouthpiece, they also compete head to head with their peers to gain an audience. The need to sell news means that they need to report on more than their identical government information—they have to provide something not only different but also better than other outlets to attract customers. Such competition has resulted in the appearance of financial experts on the media stage. Beginning as freelancers, they became institutional and government licensed. In the digital media era, the government and its licensed expert system continue to act as a powerful risk definer through active communication practices on state-owned new media platforms. However, it faces constant challenges from the privately owned social media. Due to the low level of censorship, investors who once had no right to talk through mass media suddenly found a place to voice their own opinions, viewing the existing expert system with scrutiny. They sometimes required alternative opinions in this system, a need that has stimulated the rise of unlicensed stock commentators online.

All that being said, the above is merely a rough sketch of the media stage of risk. To understand the roles that different players play on the stage, we next have to take a closer look at the important actors. People should pay attention to the internal differences among each categorized actor. For example, when we say the "Chinese government," are we referring to the People's Bank of China (PBC) or the authority of the CSRC? Are we talking about the central government, the local government, or a specific political leader from the Communist Party? All of these levels can be represented as the government, but each one actually behaves quite differently when communicating finance- or economic-related information such as financial policies and state economic statements. Similar differences exist between a financial journalist and a stock commentator, a senior commentator and a junior one, a small investor and a big fish, and so on and so forth. Moreover, though critical researchers usually focus on the tension between the government and the public, some other communicators in finance are also very influential, including listed companies, accounting firms, law firms, and securities companies. In the following chapters, I will discuss each of these players in more detail in terms of how they interact, cooperate, and confront each other on the media stage of financial risk.

The Government and the Companies

The introduction of players on the media stage started with the government, who is no doubt a major character in the risk community. It often plays the role of ruler or mass communicator, defining the social risk for the public. In some cases, however, the government becomes a potential victim of risk as well. In a nation with a strong civil society, a serious financial or economic crisis certainly can cause a disastrous political crisis (Chang, 2007). Researchers have pointed out the relationship between economics and social turmoil. For example, the 1930s Great Depression in the United States stimulated right-wing political extremism (De Bromhead et al., 2012, 2013). Similar events occurred during and after the 1997 financial crisis in Asia (Grabel, 1999; Gershman, 2002) and the 2008 debt crisis in Europe (Steinbock, 2012; Georgiadou, 2013; Matthijs, 2014). Funke, Schularick, and Trebesch (2015) examined a longer span of time, finding that "policy uncertainty rises strongly after financial crises as government majorities shrink and polarization rises." They further described the situation in the following way:

> After a crisis, voters seem to be particularly attracted to the political rhetoric of the extreme right, which often attributes blame to minorities or foreigners. On average, extreme right-wing parties increase their vote share by 30% after a financial crisis. Importantly, we do not observe similar political dynamics in normal recessions or after severe macroeconomic shocks that are not financial in nature.
>
> (p. 1)

In modern democracies, governments around the world face a difficult dilemma. When a country suffers a financial or economic shock, the government simultaneously faces polarization in parliament and public distrust. Meanwhile, the more radical parties cash in on populism and public fears, often making electoral gains. The explosion of information on social media further accelerates this situation. But how about the political impact of financial crises in an authoritarian country like China, with its omnipotent government? Before answering this question, it may be beneficial to take a close look at the past. The history of modern financial markets in China can be traced back to the 1800s, before China's Communist Party even existed. Back then, the emperor of the Qing Dynasty reigned over a feudal society, though his authority was beset with challenges from foreign intruders and colonialists. It was during that period that security markets began to develop. With the approval of Li Hongzhang, an authoritative government politician, some state-owned companies started to find financial support from the market using securities. The public's initial response was nothing short of enthusiastic, and the feudal government soon reaped the benefits of this new mechanism. The financial markets helped the government obtain money swiftly and efficiently—a vast improvement over the tax system. Though constantly disrupted by speculation, scandals, corruption, and criminal deceptions, the markets just kept expanding. The local newspaper, *Shanghai News*,[9] reported on a case that perfectly illustrates the prosperity of the stock markets during that period. In 1882, some "Western men" took the lead in developing an electric light company; to support their business, they sought to raise money from the stock market. "People all eagerly responded to the call," *Shanghai News* declared on its front page, "and those who did not buy the stocks successfully tried to trade in some from the resellers at very high prices."

The honeymoon between the imperial government and the stock markets did not last long due to the threat of financial crashes. Some of these crashes were so serious that they gained attention from the other side of the ocean. Western historical documents provide insights for today's observers into the disastrous crashes of bygone years. For example, the Consuls Reports of the United States (U.S Government Printing Office, 1891, p. 84) recorded one such crisis: "The North China News states that the Shanghai stock market has been disastrously affected by the rise in silver. Stocks of all kinds have fallen in value...."

This chaotic situation reached its peak in 1910. With the global rise of the rubber industry, locals and foreigners alike went crazy for rubber-related securities. Some bankers used China's local media to manipulate the market, portraying a glowing future for certain industries and firms, expanding the bubble even further. But the bubble eventually burst with the fall of global rubber prices, resulting in the crash of the Shanghai stock markets. The banking systems were shaken, and investors fell into mourning. Desperate, the Qing government borrowed large sums of money from foreign banks, slowing the boil temporarily. But the so-called rubber stock crisis seriously impacted the local financial system, and the seed of destruction was already planted. In 1911, to pay back its huge foreign debt, the imperial government forcefully nationalized Sichuan-Hankou Railway Company stock. Countless public shareholders were furious about their loss, and the government failed to convince the public that the policy was justified. This situation became the trigger point for the Railway Protection Movement and the Wuchang Uprising,[10] protests that eventually overthrew the Qing Dynasty. Historians continue to debate who was to blame for the social crises of the late Qing Dynasty, asserting that there may have been misunderstandings regarding risk communication between the government and the public. Worsen than that, the Qing government lacked an efficient way to communicate with the local communities. The major mouthpiece of the dynasty was "guanbao,"[11] printed official newspapers that delivered government policies and rules. They were hardly ISAs because they did not carry much ideology—the government did not use guanbao to explain or promote events, just to release their orders and decisions. During a crisis situation like the Railway Protection Movement, guanbao were by no means able to effectively seize a dominant risk definer position; they could not lead public discourse or decrease the tension between the government and the public. They tended to add fuel to the fire rather than serve as a fire extinguisher.

All in all, the Shanghai market—and by extension the Qing Dynasty itself—crashed because of a weak government lacking supervisory power, a market full of irrational speculators and cunning manipulators, and misinformation or "noise" dominating the risk communication. It demonstrates that even powerful governments are not immune to financial catastrophes. They can be removed from their position as mere rulers or controllers when people don't buy their definition of financial risk. But in the eyes of Western economists, one thing was even more fatal than the above factors. For them, what China (and other young Asian markets) lacked was simply an expert system like the experienced markets of the West. In its notes on business and finance, *The Economist*, for example, suggested "a large reform" in China's financial system, including the establishment of a clearing house (August 20, 1910, p. 383).

Almost a century later, China seems to have corrected every technical mistake regarding financial risk made by the Qing Dynasty. Without foreign colonialists, the Communist Party is far more powerful and controlling than the late Qing government. Today's China has implemented its own expert system in finance, from laws and regulations to supervising and evaluating institutions. The country's banking systems are extremely strong in the sense that they have the entire government as backup. Plus, it would be hard for investors in 1910s Shanghai to imagine the communication technologies available in the current era, all of which facilitate the spread of financial information across time and space. Today, information from the government-oriented expert system can reach the general public smoothly through different communication channels, from traditional media outlets to social media platforms. This development has eliminated the possibility for miscommunications between the government and the public based on technical issues. And of course, China has established a professional clearing house, as *The Economist* suggested a century ago.

Despite such drastic and significant changes, financial risk is endemic in China. Speculation remains excessive. Trust in supervising institutions stays low. Crashes and bubbles lurk around every corner. For many investors, the stock markets work more like casinos than legitimate institutions for raising money and sharing profits. Why is this the case? What causes expert systems to fail in dealing with financial risk? To answer this question, we arguably need to look at the biggest player in the expert system, the government, and its relationship with financial risk. Before the People's Republic of China opened its market to the world, financial risk and its consequences—economics crises, unemployment issues, and occasional financial crashes—were used to justify the rejection of capitalism's evils. More importantly, the risk was used to convince people of socialism's advantages. When China launched its new policy, it had to "distance itself from ideological orthodoxy and adopt open and reformist policies" (Chan, 2002, p. 226); meanwhile, many people opposed the embrace of a "Westernized" mechanism of finance. In 1992, even after the official opening of the SZSE and the SSE, once socialist citizens remained skeptical of capitalism in general and financial markets in particular. They were not shy about voicing their opinions of the young financial markets either: Will we suffer the same economic crises and social problems as those in the West, if we adopt a similar capitalist system of finance?

Deng Xiaoping, the former political leader of China, who had shaken hands with John Joseph Phelan, Jr.[12] six years prior, insisted that China should carry on with its economic reforms, including those to its financial system. From the viewpoint of risk definition, Deng and his supporters tried to compete with the opposing discourse of financial risk—that it is a capitalist evil that will destroy the purity of any socialist community. He justified the newborn stock markets not only by mentioning their importance but also by convincing people of the party's complete authority over financial risk:

"Securities, stock markets, are they good or bad? Are they risky or not? Are they identical to capitalism, or can socialists use them as well? ... If we are right, we run them (the financial markets) for one or two years, and we can be open to them. If we are wrong, we just correct the fault and close them."[13]

"The party can no longer close the stock market," a former fund manager told me in 2015. "There is no way back." The stock markets have become giants in China, affecting billions of people's properties and lives. In 2016, the markets had more than 3,000 listed companies[14] raising money in them, and more than 263 million valid accounts trading their securities.[15] All four of the most important national banks are listed on the market, including the Bank of China, China Construction Bank, Agricultural Bank of China, and Industrial and Commercial Bank of China. For the government, the large stamp duty tax from the markets is just a drop in the bucket compared to the money raised on the market, money that has brought the thirsty state-owned companies and banks back to life.

Ostensibly, with the PBC carrying out monetary policies and the CSRC executing supervision over the financial markets, the party government still tightly holds the reins of the stock markets. One example particularly demonstrates the government's absolute power and the market's conservative attitudes: Alibaba Group, one of the most promising e-commerce companies, could not seek an initial public offering (IPO) under China's securities law, company law, and CSRC regulations. Because its original registry place and big shareholders indicated that it was partially controlled by foreign capital, the company had to seek an IPO in the United States instead of China.[16] But even with such careful management and supervision, the interests of a highly authoritative group have become entangled with the market to such an extent that riders cannot shift the reins at will. Indeed, nowadays, even delisting one company from China's securities markets is difficult and complicated, let alone closing the market as a whole. After more than two decades, with thousands of companies passing the IPO and getting listed in China's stock markets, only 47 firms on the SSE and 54 firms on the SZSE have been removed from the market.[17] During the same period, thousands of firms were delisted from the NASDAQ and the New York Stock Exchange (NYSE). In China, some were delisted due to mergers and acquisitions. That being said, no more than 100 companies have been expelled involuntarily from the Chinese financial markets for their poor performance.

Why is this the case? It is definitely not because the rest of the listed companies have performed miraculously well. And it is not that the professionals in China fail to realize the importance of kicking the bad guys off the playground. Various individuals and institutions from the business world, academia, and the general public have called for transparency and efficiency in delisting a company from the market—this call even has been echoed by government officials themselves. There has long existed a delisting mechanism in China. The government has labeled many poorly performing companies on China's markets as "special treatment" stocks (often called ST stocks), with a ±5% daily price limit (other listed companies have a ±10% price limit)[18] They pay a special annual fee to the stock exchange, a gesture undertaken to warn investors about their high risk of being delisted. According to the 2018 version of the rules governing the listing of stocks on the SSE, articles 13.1.1 and 13.1.4, "Where an abnormality in the financial condition or other aspects of a listed company exposes the company to the risk that its stocks are likely to be terminated from listing, or makes investors unable to judge its prospects, consequently impairing their interest, the Exchange will issue a risk warning on the company's stocks...Where a delisting risk warning is issued on the stocks of a listed company, an *ST will be placed before the short name of its stock to distinguish it from other stocks." Official documents indicate that the SSE and SZSE began to place listed companies with abnormal financial statuses in a special category in 1998.[19] There have been only minor revisions in the details in the most updated versions of the rules.

Interestingly, this designation is just a yellow light, not a determinate red flag. For example, according to the rules, a company will receive a delisting warning when its "audited net profits in the most recent two consecutive financial years have been negative or remained negative upon retrospective restatement."[20] After the warning, based on 14.1.1 of the regulation, the SSE and SZSE will delist the company from the markets if its audited net profits in the most recent financial year remains negative, or if the audited operating income in the most recent financial year remains below RMB 10 million, as disclosed by the company. Certain other conditions like a material information disclosure violation might also cause the suspension of a company listing with a "yellow card."

The regulations seem to be strict and clear, but it is difficult to reconcile the fact that so few companies have been delisted from China's financial market. Many interviewees asserted that it is hard to remove a company from the market because of how it gets listed in the first place. A company needs not only fantastic performance to pass the IPO, but also good *guanxi* (Nonini & Ong, 1997) with media, bureaucrats, law firms, and accounting firms. Such *guanxi* is required to ensure that the information related to the company's performance, the *company information*, remains polished and promising. Many companies seeking an IPO have employed PR firms to coordinate *guanxi*, demonstrating its crucial nature. *Guanxi* is translated as "relationship" or "personal relationship" in English, but in China, the meaning of the word extends beyond the connection between two subjects. It indicates very complex bonds based upon exchanges of interest, and it also relates somewhat to the infamous rent-seeking scandals (see Lu, 1999; Su & Littlefield, 2001; Schramm & Taube, 2003; Szeto, Wright, & Cheng, 2006). The interactions between an ever strong political regime and a bunch of capitalists eager to enter the giant markets create an environment for under-the-table dealings with *guanxi*. Fact or fiction, the stock investors in China that I have interviewed believe that a poorly performing company can be listed purely based upon its good *guanxi* with the government and media, while a decent one failing to develop such *guanxi* can be rejected from the market. In Chapter 1, we discussed the fact that companies pay a fortune to finance companies during the IPO process in more mature financial markets. This process is like a roadshow for potential investors, demonstrating the company's solid performance and promising future. In China, the IPO is also a roadshow, with the only difference being that the "muscles" that companies show off tend to be reflections of their relationships with financial experts, the mass media, and the government in particular. This process becomes more interesting in liberal markets, because a too-close guanxi relationship with the government could be viewed suspiciously by investors. In China, however, it represents stability; it is an absolute bonus. The "real muscle" of a company loses importance, or worse, people believe that companies can fake their muscle through their guanxi as well. Ms. Li, a 49-year-old retired worker and a small investor told me this: "All in all, how can I know if a company is good or not? I do not work for that company. My daughter does not work for that company…What I know is the company's information that has been publicized. But you see, many trash companies are on the market. Don't trust them. Corruption is everywhere."

Such social corruption is not just hearsay. In 2015, for instance, one high-ranking official from the CSRC was caught when her husband invested in stock illegally. The official's duty at the institution once was related to IPO investigation. Several other officials from the CSRC who took the charge in the IPO were brought to justice as well. If the ticket to enter the market is based upon mutual benefit instead of fair evaluation, it becomes very difficult to remove a company from the market based only on performance. This fact also explains why backdoor listing, through which a company purchases a listed firm to enter into the market, is so common in China's stock market. The listed firm is a so-called shell company. Regarding this situation, a big investor, Mr. Chen, told me flatly, "People already paid the authority groups during the IPO. You see those shell companies? People *bought* the shell. They must be *used well*." In these conditions, investors often do not look down on companies labeled as "special treatment"; rather, they see it as an excuse to buy an ill performing company sometimes to keep raising money on the market. They use the nickname "rubbish companies" to describe stocks in the ST category, and they imagine that these companies are being dismissed only because they do not have guanxi with the officials. Some investors, ironically, even see an opportunity in such "rubbish companies." One big investor told me that it is "not unusual" for people to speculate on ST stocks, and even the professional fund managers are interested in doing so. "The prices (of ST stocks) are low. History tells us that there were some ST stocks that boomed after regrouping. Personally, I believe in value investment, and I would stay away from those (companies).

Regrouping may save some of the companies, but in my opinion, many ST stocks 'revived' just because of short-term speculation."

The Chinese government has been aware that the lack of public trust in company information could obstruct fluent risk communication. The CSRC, for example, claimed to be taking extreme steps to supervise financial misbehaviors, indicating that it had a "zero-tolerance" policy on corruption and bribery. It drafted regulations to conduct stricter supervision over shell companies and launched some investigations into accounting firms as well. Of course, even in the most efficient and transparent markets, improper activities like corruption, market manipulation, and *insider information* still exist and threaten the trustworthiness of risk definition, making it necessary for supervisors and rulers to step in. But as Pistor and Xu (2005) argued over ten years ago, the problem with China is that its law enforcement is not strong enough to protect investors' legal rights and punish rule breakers efficiently. A typical case was the Yinguangxia crisis of 2001. A financial magazine, *Caijing*, reported on a serious business scandal involving a listed company named Yinguangxia,[21] which was believed to have faked its financial statements to cheat the market. The investors had been misled by false company information and were of course furious. But on September 21, 2001, the Chinese Supreme People's Court (CSPC) released a notice entitled "Civil Lawsuits about Stock Investments are Temporarily not Acceptable," banning the local courts from accepting such lawsuits from stock investors.[22] The reason for this ruling was that the laws—one decade after the market's birth—were not yet clear and complete enough to justify such lawsuits.

After the Central People's Government passed the securities laws in 2005, the legal system became stronger. But almost all the investors I interviewed insisted that legal insurance remains limited for them, particularly considering the existence of a large amount of false company information that hurts investors in the Chinese stock market. To be fair, some of these beliefs rely on hearsay or imagination, with no hard evidence, but it is real for *them*.

The Everbright case mentioned in Chapter 1 provides another example. The Everbright Company knew that the extraordinary surge in stock prices resulted from a buying error in its digital trading system, but it did not release this information to the public in a timely fashion. Instead, the company publicly denied the accident, misleading other investors and the government while privately using a hedge strategy to reduce its own risk. Foreseeing the market purge, it sold off large amounts of exchange-traded funds (ETF, a type of index fund) and short sold the stock index futures to make up for its own loss (Xie, 2016).

The lawsuits against Everbright Securities illustrate the progress that Chinese government has made in protecting investors from being misled regarding risk communication. Nonetheless, investors still believe that such insurance remains case-based and uncertain. They don't understand why to wait the notice from the Supreme People's Court before they can sue the company. In general, this event encapsulates the relationship between the government and financial risk: Both the authorities and the public still believe in the power of the socialist government as a determinate ruler of the financial markets. This viewpoint is apparent in the fact that during the Everbright crisis, many investors failed to question the SSE's declaration through social media that the market was "normal." They believed that positive news on the government level could affect the market to that extent. But the absolute power of the government/party and its partial adoption of capitalism resulted not in liberalization but in the rise of a corrupt "cadre-capitalist class" (Nonini, 2008). People observed, imagined, or believed in collusions or *guanxi* between the cadre and the big capitalists, and they started to question the transparency, legitimacy, and professionalism of the officials defining financial risk for them. Any information coming from the government is still considered extremely important, but people would also listen to their doubts. It may take time for the government to build up public trust and play a dominant role in defining risk for investors.

Concerning the *company information*, the government's risk position is that of a supervisor: It is supposed to guarantee the communication of accurate facts about a company, and punish any misleading communicators. But the government plays a different role when communicating the information like national policies or national economic reports, which I call *national affairs*. When releasing information about *national affairs*, the government becomes not the supervisor but the major communicator. Regarding such information, the investors I interviewed portrayed the government as a strong figure, and some of their imaginings would be bizarre in the eyes of free-market liberals. For example, a small investor Mr. Huang once told me that "it is a good idea to invest in the stock market before the Chinese New Year, because the government will release some good national news and buoy up the market to keep us *laobaixing*[23] happy." When the stock market crashes before festivals, some investors become truly angry at the government. Such investors may be easily regarded as irrational and incapable, but their strange perceptions of the government do not emerge from a vacuum. They are based upon their long-term experiences in a society in transition, one where the government still dominates many social aspects, including the financial market. Ironically, the Qing Dynasty's weakness posed a risk to the market hundreds of years ago, while today's investors somehow associate the current government's power with uncertainty.

Financial Journalists and Stock Commentators

In addition to the government, people who work for media outlets to talk and write about financial issues play a crucial role on the media stage of risk. These communicators can be categorized into two categories in terms of their expertise: media experts and stock commentators.

The former group primarily includes financial journalists and editors from various media outlets and newsrooms. Their roles, duties, and limitations coincide with other journalists in China, except for the fact that they focus on financial issues instead of other social dimensions. Regarding government policies, they simply deliver the relevant information swiftly and correctly. On the other hand, they tend to have more wiggle room when it comes to company news. Most of the media experts I interviewed are proud to perform a supervisory role over the market; they view their work as a service for the government and the public. The editor of a financial newspaper, Mr. Zhang, told me that "being professional and critical" is the goal of his team. A financial journalist, Miss Chen, agreed: "Aside from providing decent reviews and predictions (of the market), we also supervise the companies for the government and investors." With confidence, she cited *Caijing's* reporting on the Yinguangxia crisis as an example: "We have good companies, and there are also bad ones. We need to reveal the truth. Throw a red flag, you know."

Although media experts identify themselves as critical supervisors and professional analysts, other players in the risk communication game do not concur. On China's social media, business people, lawyers, media employees, and PR companies openly complain that some media outlets blackmail companies with IPOs. A common media trick is to ask a company to buy advertisements and services from them, or even directly ask for bribes. If the company refuses to do so, the media releases negative reports on the company, preventing it from passing the IPO. A media expert in China described the situation as "an open secret." One CEO openly stated that a company under IPO must pay at least "three to ten million" Chinese Yuan to develop the *guanxi* necessary to satisfy blackmailers. Such corruption corrodes the trustworthiness of *company information* released by the media while producing uncertainty for the whole market. Mr. Zhang, the editor, denied that his outlet has anything to do with the scandals, and pointed a finger at the companies claiming to be blackmailed. "There is no smoke without fire. If the news reports are correct, they indicate that the companies are problematic. The companies should think about what they have done wrong first." But he also admitted that "it is not impossible" that some of his media peers might partake in corruption. He told me, "It really hurts to think that the media's reputation has been damaged like this." Ironically, the definers and reporters of risk thus have become producers of risk under certain circumstances.

Apart from these editors and journalists, *stock commentators* are another group of people who must rely on media outlets to communicate financial information. Miss Chen explained the difference between her work as a journalist and as a stock commentator to me as follows: "We financial journalists focus on the facts, while those commentators need to provide more than that." An investor might not care who wrote a piece of financial news, but the same does not hold true when watching, listening to, or reading a piece of *stock commentary*: In this case, the messenger's name is of the utmost importance. A small investor living in Shanghai told me that he continues to subscribe to a Sichuan newspaper named "Finance and Investment." Even though Shanghai has numerous similar newspapers and magazines, he chooses "Finance and Investment" because his favorite stock commentator writes for that Sichuan newspaper. One of the few types of information that is important to investors, stock commentary helps them to evaluate their investment risks. Some stock commentators continue to enjoy strong reputations today, and people like to hear their perspectives. As a group, however, stock commentators are infamous in China with several sharp critics. The investors call them "black mouths" or "black-hearted commentators." Mr. Huang, a small investor, directly identified a stock commentator and said, "He's a liar." As this example shows, their professional credentials are doubted, and their honesty is questioned—but it was not always so.

As Mr. Gao, a famous stock commentator working in the field for over two decades, told me, "That was not the case back in the 1990s. Stock commentators were celebrities back then ... Those were the good old days. We were like outlaws in Water Margin.[24] Your fighting skills determined your reputation in Water Margin. In the stock market, the money you earned and your investment talent determined your reputation (being a stock commentator). No one could fake that. The investors knew your quality. They made the good ones famous. You know what, people paid to listen to our talks." Mr. Gao referred to Water Margin, a Chinese story about 108 outlaws who developed their own army, fighting against the government during the Song Dynasty. These Chinese Robin Hoods enjoy timeless affection due to their rebellious spirits and desire for freedom. At the end of their story, the Water Margin outlaws were granted amnesty from the government, but many of them met with tragic ends nonetheless. For Mr. Gao, the same storyline exists for the old stock commentators.

"At the end of the 1990s, the government launched examinations for the stock commentators. Only those who were licensed could release stock commentary in the media. Do you think those examinations can truly tell who is good and who is bad? Nonsense. Look at the current commentators, and you know how ridiculous the mechanism is." He pointed out to me that after institutionalization, the standards for being a stock commentator changed, and the commentators as a group became a source of trouble rather than an opinion leader in risk communication. However, Mr. Zeng, one of "those current commentators," protested fiercely to me. "The license is a must-have. Basic knowledge, basic knowledge. Without the examinations, who knows if you know general knowledge of the stock market? The government is right. In my eyes, they should even do more to regulate the stock commentary market."

In Chapter 6, we will further examine *stock commentary* and revisit the debate between Mr. Gao and Mr. Zeng. But beforehand, let's take another look at the full picture of risk communication. All of the professional institutions mentioned above—from the government to the accounting firms, law firms, and news outlets—constitute what is called an expert system in finance. Taken together, they ideally guarantee upright, efficient, and transparent risk communication regarding the stock market while ensuring positive relations between the most promising companies and the public. They are supposed to identify what is risky and what is secure, portraying a genuine and comprehensive picture of a market or a company for the general public. However, public distrust harms the expert system's overall power to provide risk definition in finance. The dismantling in professionalism removes these experts—most of whom are institutional professionals—from their absolutely dominant position in defining risk. They are still considered important sources of information, but the truth of their statements is no longer taken for granted. Some individual, semi-institutional, or institutional players, AKA big "bankers" and small investors (sanhu), therefore have stepped up to a more central place on the stage with the equipment of information and communication technologies (ICTs). They refuse to blindly follow the communication of financial risk by the government-oriented expert system; instead, they communicate and calculate uncertainty using their own philosophies and strategies. Interestingly, though they collectively have created an alternative to the expert system of financial communication, the small investors and big bankers usually are regarded as "enemies" in China. The last section of this chapter explores the complicated relationships between them.

Big "Bankers" vs. Small Investors

An investor told me during the interview, that in China's stock market, "the big fish eat the small fish, and the small fish eat even smaller shrimps." This metaphor reveals the zero-sum culture in the financial world, as well as the high level of tension between those who take advantage of others and those who are taken advantage of. It also indicates the flexible and changeable positions of the stock market; the advantaged investors may be at risk when facing more powerful players. Based on this belief, people try to draw clear lines between the powerful groups, less powerful groups, and subordinate groups. One way to do so is to divide the investors based purely on their capital. For example, those who invest less than 100 thousand CNY in the market are the smaller shrimps, or small investors. Those who own 100 thousand to 500 thousand CNY are small fish, or middle investors. And those who own above that range are big investors. Mr. Chen, a millionaire investor, does not agree with categorizing investors in this manner. "It's just relative. I am a big investor in the eyes of those sanhu, sure. But compared to the big funds, I am nothing...Over 500 thousand CNY (to be a big investor)? Ha, you must be kidding me."

But generally speaking, though it lacks strict criteria, being a "big investor" is not a completely flexible concept. In China, this group has the nickname of "big bankers" (zhuangjia), which may offer a clue about what distinguishes the big investors from the small ones. The Chinese word for banker (zhuangjia) frequently appeared in China's social discourse before 1949, ordinarily referring to those in charge of banks or casinos. Following the birth of the People's Republic of China in 1949, the prior financial system vanished, and the gambling industry was forbidden in the socialist country. During the first decades of the Communist Party's governance, a pure and innocent socialist period, the term "banker" ideologically disappeared in social discourse. Indeed, the word was not mentioned in the *People's Daily*, the mouthpiece newspaper of the Chinese government, from 1949 to the mid-1980s. It was not until the 1990s, with the opening of the stock market, that the term "bankers" again began to appear regularly in China's news outlets. People regard the big investors as a combination of card sharks and bankers in a gambling game. *People's Daily*, for example, defines big bankers as those who "communicate insider information or manipulate the market" (Tian, 1998, p. 20). They are a priority group in capital, capable of influencing the stock price on their own; at the very least, they are able to do so in cooperation with others. But their most impressive characteristic is their manipulating of the market with communication to take advantage of misled small shrimps. They could be institutional or semi-institutional players, like formal fund managers, or informal traders who invest for the big capitalists. Some of them work on their own in the market.

Even the most experienced investors I interviewed, among whom were the first stock investors in China, did not remember whom was first to call the big investors "bankers." Some investors suggested that the label might come from people's impressions of the deceptive "bankers" in those 80s and 90s Hong Kong gangster movies. Whatever the reason, big investors became the bankers "with Chinese characteristics," the opposite of which were small investors, AKA the "small sanhu" in Chinese. "San" means scattered, while "hu" means accounts. Unlike many markets in the Global North, China's absolute amount of sanhu-owned capital outnumbered that of the big capitalists without question, a condition that makes it difficult for big capitalists to wield control over the market as easily as they once did. But due to the scattering of small investors, it is impossible for them to act collectively on a regular basis, meaning that they are not able to intentionally impact the market like big investors.

This inequality between the "bankers" and the sanhu, or the fact that most individual investors hold more risk than wealthy ones, is not news in the financial world. Over a century ago, Max Weber (2000 [1894]) researched London stock markets and revealed that stock market dangers definitely involved class: The workers were more vulnerable to stock risk because of their weak economic status, and they were more likely to be convinced by false information about stock returns. Compared to the workers, Weber said, "the big capitalist, when criticized, points to the 'disreputable elements' who take part in trading on the exchanges" (Weber, 2000 [1894], p. 333). Weber then made two suggestions regarding stock market development. First, he called for stronger regulation and supervision of stock exchanges to prevent investor exploitation in the capitalist world. And second, he believed that unprofessional individuals should be banned from the market to avoid such risks.

The history of stock markets in the now developed countries seems to align with Weber's two suggestions. Take the U.S. stock market as an example. In the 1930s, the U.S. securities law was launched, the "backbone" of which was to protect small investors from abuses in the financial markets (Zingales, 2012, p. 233). Today, people barely talk about the original purpose of such regulations. In the 1920s, finance professor Luigi Zingales (2012) wrote, "Individuals owned 90 percent of publicly traded equity. By 2007, that figure had dropped to less than 30 percent." The management and communication of financial risk have been institutionalized because professional funds took over control of capital in the market for individuals. The exclusion of individual investors from the finance discussion does not seem to be coercive but voluntary, in that it prevents the incapables from facing exposure to risk. The experts celebrated this tendency, claiming that it benefits the economy as a whole (Hawley & Williams, 2000). This transformation in the financial world, however, was followed by the emergence of new inequities. When people hand over their money to expert institutional systems, they also hand over the power to define risk in finance, which devalues, if not shuts down, their own evaluations of publicly traded companies. On the other hand, by seizing the power to define risk, Wall Streeters and other actors in this expert system have created fortunes based on their agency in calculating financial risk (and chance) for the general public. Although people may question whether their fortunes are reasonable, or whether their decisions regarding risk have been righteous, professional-oriented risk cultures have been established and are now entrenched in the Global North.

As for the stock markets in China, it seems that they are going through the same process as London and U.S. financial markets in their early days: Market assessments are extremely equitable, and the handling of risk is very individualized. At various points, small investors have reaped the fruits of the flourishing economy and publicly traded firms without handing over huge commissions to experts. Opening an account in a stock company requires only a Chinese ID, a bank account, and a registration fee of usually less than 100 CNY. An investor could invest the least amount in the cheapest stock in the Chinese market (as calculated on April 20, 2010) for only 359 CNY (Xiao, 2010). In 2012, this figure was equivalent to 1.46% of the average disposable income per year for urban residents and 4.54% of the annual income for rural residents.[25] The bull market period in China, from the middle of 2006 until the end of 2007, led to a major increase in many investors' incomes, which may have facilitated people's mobility from lower classes to upper classes (Zhang, 2004; Yao & Luo, 2009). But simultaneously, as discussed above, small investors claim to be extremely vulnerable to financial risk. In addition to illegal activities in the stock market, national and global economic conditions also cause risk in the Chinese stock market, as can be seen from the 2007 U.S. economic crisis, the 2008 EU debt crisis, and the downturn of China's own economy in recent years (Zhang, 2010). After reaching a peak of 6124.04 in October of 2007, the Shanghai Composite Index has entered a period of decline. By December 2012, the lowest Shanghai Composite Index was about 1,950 points. The same scenario occurred in the SSE. The highest point in the compositional index of the Shenzhen Stock Market was 19600.03, which also occurred in October 2007. In December 2012, the lowest point of its compositional index was 7660.45. According to the CSRC, billions of dollars have been invested in the stock market over the past five years, and the majority of individual investors in China have lost a large amount of money. General Office of the State Council of China declares that, apart from the large-scale economic crises or unpredictable financial crashes, like the Everbright crisis, small investors claim to have suffered the most from excessive day-to-day speculation in the stock market. The Office of the State Council encouraged government institutions to view protecting small investors' legal interests as the "foundation" of sustainable and healthy development in the Chinese capital market. The Chinese government, like the U.S. government in the 1930s, decided to use securities law to protect small investors from risk.

And now, China is standing at a crossroads: Will it repeat the history of the U.S. stock market, institutionalizing the definition and management of financial risk? Will it restrict equal access to risk communication to ensure stability? The government-licensed expert system seems to support the latter path. They are now testing the waters to see if they can persuade the government to legitimately exclude the sanhu from the market under the guise of protecting them from themselves. But based on my observations of the current financial markets in China, I can draw a safe conclusion that the big and small investors in China has collectively produced unique philosophies or, in other words, *risk cultures* regarding financial risk, which will be the biggest obstacle to the institutionalization of financial markets. These cultures differ from the historical processes undertaken in the United States, and they form the biggest barriers faced by the government in institutionalizing risk management. Such cultures favor private information over public discourse, and *guanxi* over contractual relations. They cause excessive speculation on the surface and *individualization of risk* underneath, as Chinese investors would rather stick to a more personalized method of financial trading rather than turning to an institution for help. The individualization of risk here actually has little to do with individualism. Instead of dealing with uncertainty alone, Chinese investors collectively have developed small-scale networks in response to risk communication. Financial experts may conclude that this practice results purely from the irrationality of the unprofessional Chinese investors, suggesting that their greed surpasses their logic. But if one takes a closer look at the communicative practices of these investors when exchanging different types of information, they may reach an altogether different conclusion. Indeed, as the upcoming chapters illustrate, every step is based upon the investors' deliberate use of communication technologies, observations of China's social and political mechanisms, and unwavering belief in the roles of different actors in staging financial risk.

Those communication practices of the investors, however, are at almost a very soft version of protest against, or merely a complaint of, the hierarchies in financial world. On-street demonstrations, open political outcries, and other common forms of actions we have noticed in social movements did not happen with regard to the participants of financial investments. That might be the reason why most of the critical researchers neglect financial worlds, with a conclusion that nothing rebellious is happening there. But ironically, that is also the reason why the Chinese government has taken a comparatively tolerant attitude toward financial communication online. Under such constancies, people have talked about financial information through numerous blogs, microblogs, forum posts, and group chats on a daily basis, and they insist to do the trading orders by themselves through stock investment APPs and software. And eventually the online "noises" became louder than the voices those "experts" have made, which had no real threat at most of the time to the political regime, but indeed created a social space alternative to the government-oriented or licensed expert system, forming a unique risk culture in China's financial world.

Notes

1 One example is Blue Ocean Network (BON TV), a privately owned TV station in China which only provides programs abroad.
2 See http://tv.cctv.com/cctv2/
3 See http://www.yicai.com/
4 See http://paper.xinhuanet.com/zgzqb.html

5 The types of information mentioned in this chapter will be discussed further in the proceeding chapters, including company information, stock quotes, national affairs, insider information, and stock commentary.

6 For more details about Sun's case, see Hand (2006, 2009).

7 Many provinces/cities in China have removed the temporary living permit system from 2003 (Shi, Chen & Wang, 2016).

8 http://dtdg777.blog.163.com/

9 Also known as *Shen Bao*, a once influential newspaper published in Shanghai from 1872 to 1949.

10 Both were political protest movements during the late Qing Dynasty.

11 To learn more about guanbao, see Wagner (2008), Kun (2011), and Vittinghoff (2002).

12 Former president and chairman of the NYSE.

13 See Chen, T., Chen, J., & Niu, Z., (1992). The documentary of Xiaoping Deng in Shenzhen. *The People's Daily*, 1.

14 Until November 30, 2016, data retrieved from the CSRC.

15 Until October 30, 2016, data retrieved from the CSRC.

16 This is not to say that no foreign-controlled firms can seek IPOs in China, but it depends on the nature of the firm, and overall, it's very difficult. China's authorities have mentioned that they may ease such constraints a bit in 2017.

17 Data from the Shanghai Stock Exchange and Shenzhen Stock Exchange, 2017, available at http://www.sse.com.cn/assortment/stock/list/delisting/ and https://www.szse.cn/main/marketdata/jypz/ztzzssgs/

18 The data has been retrieved from http://english.sse.com.cn/investors/ shhkconnect/mechanism/rules/. To know more about ST design in China's stock market, see Jiang, Lee, and Yue (2010), Eun and Huang (2007), and Chen, Lee, and Li (2008) for reference.

19 See   http://english.sse.com.cn/aboutsse/sseoverview/historical/c/c_20151130_ 4017197.shtml

20 The Exchange will issue a delisting risk warning for the stocks of a listed company upon the occurrence of any of the following circumstances: (1) its audited net profits in the two most recent consecutive financial years have been negative or remained negative upon retrospective restatement; (2) its audited net assets at the end of the most recent financial year are or remain negative upon retrospective restatement; (3) its audited revenues in the most recent financial year are less than RMB 10,000,000 or remain less than RMB 10 million upon retrospective restatement; (4) its financial report for the most recent financial year is issued a disclaimer of opinion or adverse opinion by a CPA firm; (5) it has been ordered by the CSRC to correct serious errors or falsehoods in its financial report but fails to mend its ways within the specified time limit, and its stocks have been suspended from trading for two months; (6) it fails to disclose its annual report or interim report within the statutory period, and its stocks have been suspended from trading for two months; (7) after its equity structure as prescribed in Article 12.14 hereof renders it unsuitable for listing, it submits to the Exchange a plan for addressing the equity structure problem within the required one-month period and obtains approval from the Exchange; (8) it is under an administrative sanction by the CSRC for any misrepresentations, misleading statements, or material omissions in its IPO application or disclosure documents, which makes it an unqualified issuer fraudulently obtaining IPO approval or has a material impact on the offering pricing of new stocks, or is referred to the public security authority for the suspected commission of the crime of fraudulent offering (hereinafter, fraudulent offering); (9) it is

under an administrative sanction by the CSRC for any misrepresentations, misleading statements, or material omissions in its disclosure documents and is determined in the decision of such administrative sanction to have committed a material violation of laws because of the serious nature, severity, and significant impact on the market of such violation, or is referred to the public security authority for the suspected commission of a disclosure violation or the crime of nondisclosure of material information (hereinafter, material information disclosure violation); (10) it is likely to be forced to dissolve; (11) a court has accepted its application for reorganization, settlement, or bankruptcy liquidation; and (12) other circumstances as recognized by the Exchange. For more details, see http://english.sse.com.cn/laws/framework/c/4547752.pdf

21 The Yinguangxia crisis will be discussed in details in Chapter 5.

22 See CSPC, notice number 406.

23 *Laobaixing* means ordinary people or the general public in Chinese (Zhang, 2004; Chen & Mehndiratta, 2007).

24 Water Margin is a classic novel in Chinese literature. The story happened during the Song Dynasty.

25 According to the data from the National Bureau of Statistics of China.

References

Alexander, P. (2010). Rebellion of the poor: South Africa's service delivery protests—a preliminary analysis. *Review of African Political Economy*, *37*(123), 25–40.

Alexander, P., & Pfaffe, P. (2014). Social relationships to the means and ends of protest in South Africa's ongoing rebellion of the poor: The Balfour insurrections. *Social Movement Studies*, *13*(2), 204–221.

Althusser, L. (2006). Ideology and ideological state apparatuses (notes towards an investigation). *The Anthropology of the State: A Reader*, *9*(1), 86–98.

Arouri, M., & Liu, C. (2008). Stock craze: An empirical analysis of PER in Chinese equity market. *Economics Bulletin*, *1*(14), 1–17.

Bai, R. (2005). Media commercialization, entertainment, and the party-state: The political economy of contemporary Chinese television entertainment culture. *Global Media Journal*, *4*(6), 1–54.

Beck, U. (1992). *Risk society: Towards a new modernity*. London: Sage.

Bian, J. (2014). *China's securities market: Towards efficient regulation* (Vol. 2). New York: Routledge.

Chan, J. M. (2002). Disneyfying and globalizing the Chinese legend Mulan: A study of transculturation. In J. M. Chan & B. T. McIntyre (Eds.) *In search of boundaries: Communication, nation-states and cultural identities* (pp. 225–248). Westport, CT: Ablex.

Chan, J. M., & Qiu, J. L. (2002). Media liberalization under authoritarianism. In M. E. Price, B. Rozumilowicz, & S. G. Verhulst (Eds.) *Media reform: Democratizing the media, democratizing the state* (pp. 27–46). London and New York: Routledge.

Chang, R. (2007). Financial crises and political crises. *Journal of Monetary Economics*, *54*(8), 2409–2420.

Chen, X. (2007). On party newspaper's dominant role and its marginalization in operating. *Asian Social Science*, *4*(1), 83.

Chen, X., Lee, C. W. J., & Li, J. (2008). Government assisted earnings management in China. *Journal of Accounting and Public Policy, 27*(3), 262–274.

Chen, W., & Mehndiratta, S. (2007). Planning for Laobaixing: Public participation in urban transportation project, Liaoning, China. *Transportation Research Record: Journal of the Transportation Research Board, 1994*, 128–137.

Cheng, H. (2008). Insider trading in China: The case for the Chinese Securities Regulatory Commission. *Journal of Financial Crime, 15*(2), 165–178.

Davies, J. C. (1962). Toward a theory of revolution. *American Sociological Review, 27*(1), 5–19.

De Bromhead, A., Eichengreen, B., & O'Rourke, K. H. (2012). Right-wing political extremism in the Great Depression (No. w17871). National Bureau of Economic Research.

De Bromhead, A., Eichengreen, B., & O'Rourke, K. H. (2013). Political extremism in the 1920s and 1930s: Do German lessons generalize? *The Journal of Economic History, 73*(2), 371–406.

Eun, C. S., & Huang, W. (2007). Asset pricing in China's domestic stock markets: Is there a logic? *Pacific-Basin Finance Journal, 15*(5), 452–480.

Fu, K. W., Chan, C. H., & Chau, M. (2013). Assessing censorship on microblogs in China: Discriminatory keyword analysis and the real-name registration policy. *IEEE Internet Computing, 17*(3), 42–50.

Funke, M., Schularick, M., & Trebesch, C. (2015). *Politics in the slump: Polarization and extremism after financial crises, 1870–2014*. Unpublished, Free University of Berlin.

Gang, Q., & Bandurski, D. (2011). China's emerging public sphere: The impact of media commercialization, professionalism, and the Internet in an era of transition. In Susan Shrik (Ed.) *Changing media, changing China* (pp. 38–76). New York: Oxford University Press.

Georgiadou, V. (2013). Right-wing populism and extremism: The rapid rise of "Golden Dawn" in crisis-ridden Greece. *Right-wing extremism in Europe, 75*.

Gershman, J. (2002). Is Southeast Asia the second front? *Foreign affairs, 81*(4), 60–74.

Grabel, I. (1999). Rejecting exceptionalism—reinterpreting the Asian financial crises. In J. Michie & J. G. Smith (Eds.) *Global instability* (pp. 37–67). London: Routledge.

Guo, Z., Chan, K. C., & Huang, J. (2017). Can media coverage restrain executive empire building and pursuit of a quiet life? Evidence from China. *International Review of Economics & Finance, 56*, 547–563.

Habermas, J. (1989). *The structural transformation of the public sphere*, trans. T. Burger. Cambridge: MIT Press, 85, 85–92.

Habermas, J. (1996). Civil society and the political public sphere. In W. Rehg (Trans.), *Between facts and norms – Contributions to a discourse theory of law and democracy* (pp. 329–387). Cambridge: Polity Press.

Habermas, J. (2001). The public sphere: An encyclopedia article. In M. G. Durham & D. Kellner (Eds.), *Media and cultural studies: Keyworks* (pp. 102–107). Oxford: Blackwell.

Han, L. (2011). "Lucky cloud" over the world: The journalistic discourse of nationalism beyond China in the Beijing Olympics global torch relay. *Critical Studies in Media Communication, 28*(4), 275–291.

Hand, K. J. (2006). Using law for a righteous purpose: The Sun Zhigang incident and evolving forms of citizen action in the People's Republic of China. *Columbia Journal of Transnational Law, 45*, 114.

Hand, K. J. (2009). Citizens engage the constitution: The Sun Zhigang incident and constitutional review proposals in the People's Republic of China. In S. Balme & M. W. Dowdle (Eds.), *Building constitutionalism in China* (pp. 221–242). New York: Palgrave Macmillan.

Hassid, J. (2012). Safety valve or pressure cooker? Blogs in Chinese political life. *Journal of Communication, 62*(2), 212–230.

Hawley, J. P., & Williams, A. T. (2000). *The rise of fiduciary capitalism: How institutional investors can make corporate America more democratic.* Philadelphia: University of Pennsylvania Press.

Herold, D. K. (2008). Development of a civic society online?: Internet vigilantism and state control in Chinese cyberspace. *Asia Journal of Global Studies, 2*(1), 26–37.

Hong, J. (1998a). *The internationalization of television in China: The evolution of ideology, society, and media since the reform.* Westport, CT: Greenwood Publishing Group.

Hong, L. (1998b). Profit or ideology? The Chinese press between party and market. *Media, Culture & Society, 20*(1), 31–41.

Hung, C. F. (2003). Public discourse and "virtual" political participation in the PRC: The impact of the Internet. *Issues & Studies, 39*(4), 1–38.

Jiang, G., Lee, C. M., & Yue, H. (2010). Tunneling through intercorporate loans: The China experience. *Journal of Financial Economics, 98*(1), 1–20.

King, G., Pan, J., & Roberts, M. E. (2013). How censorship in China allows government criticism but silences collective expression. *American Political Science Review, 107*(2), 326–343.

Kun, W. E. I. (2011). Exploration of the features and sources of the tabloid in song dynasty. *Journal of Wuhan University of Technology (Social Sciences Edition), 5*, 014.

Lagerkvist, J. (2012). Principal-agent dilemma in China's social media sector? The party-state and industry real-name registration waltz. *International Journal of Communication, 6*, 19.

Latham, K. (2000). Nothing but the truth: News media, power and hegemony in South China. *The China Quarterly, 163*, 633–654.

Lee, C. C., He, Z., & Huang, Y. (2007). Party-market corporatism, clientelism, and media in Shanghai. *Harvard International Journal of Press/Politics, 12*(3), 21–42.

Li, X., Xuan, Q., & Kluver, R. (2003). The impact of online chatrooms on party presses in China. In K. C. Ho, R. Kluver, & K. Yang (Eds.), *Asia.com: Asia encounters the Internet* (p. 143). London: RoutledgeCurzon.

Li, Y., & Long, Q. (2017). Reconstructing hegemony in the context of new media: The Weibo account of People's Daily and its communicational adaptation (2012–2014). *Communication & Society, 39*, 157–187.

Liu, Q., & McCormick, B. (2011). The media and the public sphere in contemporary China. *Boundary 2, 38*(1), 101–134.

Lu, X. (1999). From rank-seeking to rent-seeking: Changing administrative ethos and corruption in reform China. *Crime, Law and Social Change, 32*(4), 347–370.

Lu, X. (2004). *Rhetoric of the Chinese cultural revolution: The impact on Chinese thought, culture, and communication.* Columbia, SC: University of South Carolina Press.

Ma, Q. (2003). *The history of China's securities: 1978–1998.* China: Zhongxin Press.

MacKinnon, R. (2011). China's "networked authoritarianism". *Journal of Democracy, 22*(2), 32–46.

Matthijs, M. (2014). Mediterranean blues: The crisis in Southern Europe. *Journal of Democracy, 25*(1), 101–115.

Nonini, D. M. (2008). Is China becoming neoliberal? *Critique of Anthropology, 28*(2), 145–176.

Nonini, D. M., & Ong, A. (1997). Chinese transnationalism as an alternative modernity. In A. Ong & D. Nonini (Eds.) *Ungrounded empires: The cultural politics of modern Chinese transnationalism* (pp. 3–33). London: Routledge.

Özerdem, A., & Podder, S. (2012). Grassroots and rebellion: A study on the future of the Moro struggle in Mindanao, Philippines. *Civil Wars, 14*(4), 521–545.

Parsons, P., & Xu, X. (2001). News framing of the Chinese embassy bombing by the People's Daily and the New York Times. *Asian Journal of Communication, 11*(1), 51–67.

Pistor, K., & Xu, C. (2005). Governing stock markets in transition economies: Lessons from China. *American Law and Economics Review, 7*(1), 184–210.

Qiang, X. (2004). The rising tide of Internet opinion in China. *Nieman Reports, 58*(2), 103.

Qiu, L. & Chan, J. M. (2009). Approaching new media events research. *Communication and Society, 3*(2), 19–37.

Schiller, D. (2000). *Digital capitalism.* Cambridge, MA: MIT Press.

Schramm, M., & Taube, M. (2003). The institutional economics of legal institutions, Guanxi, and corruption in the PR China. In *Fighting corruption in Asia: Causes, effects and remedies* (pp. 271–296). Singapore: World Scientific Publishing.

Shi, W., Chen, J., & Wang, H. (2016). Affordable housing policy in China: New developments and new challenges. *Habitat International, 54*, 224–233.

Sima, Y. (2011). Grassroots environmental activism and the Internet: Constructing a green public sphere in China. *Asian Studies Review, 35*(4), 477–497.

Steinbock, D. (2012). The Eurozone debt crisis: Prospects for Europe, China, and the United States. *American Foreign Policy Interests, 34*(1), 34–42.

Su, C., & Littlefield, J. E. (2001). Entering guanxi: A business ethical dilemma in mainland China? *Journal of Business Ethics, 33*(3), 199–210.

Sukosd, M., & Wang, L. (2013). From centralization to selective diversification: A historical analysis of media structure and agency in China, 1949–2013. *Journal of Media Business Studies, 10*(4), 83–104.

Szeto, R., Wright, P. C., & Cheng, E. (2006). Business networking in the Chinese context: Its role in the formation of guanxi, social capital and ethical foundations. *Management Research News, 29*(7), 425–438.

The Economist (1910, August 20). The Shanghai crisis. *The Economist Historical Archive, 1843–2011*, 383. Accessed February 13, 2017.

Tian, J. (1998, November 9). Securities Law is good news. *People's Daily*, 10.

U.S. Government Printing Office. (1891). United States Consular Reports: Reports from the Consuls of the United States on the commerce, manufactures, etc., of their consular districts. Retrieved from https://books.google.com.hk/books/about/United_States_Consular_Reports.html?id=rhxJAQAAIAAJ&redir_esc=y

Vittinghoff, N. (2002). Unity vs. uniformity: Liang Qichao and the invention of a "new journalism" for China. *Late Imperial China, 23*(1), 91–143.

Wagner, R. G. (Ed.). (2008). *Joining the global public: Word, image, and city in early Chinese newspapers, 1870–1910*. Albany: State University New York Press.

Wallis, C. (2011). New media practices in China: Youth patterns, processes, and politics. *International Journal of Communication, 5*, 31.

Weber, M. (2000, originally published in 1984). Stock and commodity exchanges. *Theory and Society, 29*, 305–338.

Wu, Y. (2007). Blurring boundaries in a "Cyber-Greater China": Are Internet bulletin boards constructing the public sphere in China? In R. Butsch (Ed.), *Media and public spheres* (pp. 210–222). London: Palgrave Macmillan.

Xiao, Li. (2010, April 21). Bring the stock investment to the rural area. *East Morning Daily*. Retrieved from http://finance.sina.com.cn/stock/y/20100421/01397793195.shtml

Xie, J. (2016). Criminal regulation of high frequency trading on China's capital markets. *International Journal of Law, Crime and Justice, 47*, 106–120.

Yang, G. (2006). Activists beyond virtual borders: Internet-mediated networks and informational politics in China. *First Monday, 7*. Retrieved from http://firstmonday.org/issues/special11_9/yang

Yang, G. (2013). Contesting food safety in the Chinese media: Between hegemony and counter-hegemony. *The China Quarterly, 214*, 337–355.

Yang, G., & Calhoun, C. (2007). Media, civil society, and the rise of a green public sphere in China. *China Information, 21*(2), 211–236.

Yao, S., & Luo, D. (2009). The economic psychology of stock market bubbles in China. *The World Economy, 32*(5), 667–691.

Yu, H. (2006). From active audience to media citizenship: The case of post-Mao China. *Social Semiotics, 16*(2), 303–326.

Zhang, S. (2010, March 22). Eastmoney.com became a listed company and entered the market. *Shanghai Business*. Retrieved from http://www.shbiz.com.cn/

Zhang, Y. (2004). Styles, subjects, and special points of view: A study of contemporary Chinese independent documentary. *New Cinemas: Journal of Contemporary Film, 2*(2), 119–136.

Zhao, Y. (1998). *Media, market, and democracy in China: Between the party line and the bottom line* (vol. 137). Champaign: University of Illinois Press.

Zheng, Y., & Wu, G. (2005). Information technology, public space, and collective action in China. *Comparative Political Studies, 38*(5), 507–536.

Zhu, Y. (2006). Proclamation, implementation, and abolishment of China's custody and repatriation law—an institutionalist analysis. *American Journal of Chinese Studies, 13*(2), 187–208.

Zingales, L. (2012). *Capitalism for the people: Recapturing the lost genius of American prosperity*. New York: Basic Books.

3 Communicating Stock Quotes

Chapter 2 introduces the major players communicating and constructing financial risk. Following this discussion, the chapter turns to the detailed communication practices of two groups of major players, small investors (sanhu) and big bankers (zhuangjia). The traditional mass communication model would regard them (especially those *sanhu*) as passive receivers of the message coming from the expert finance system. In reality, however, these players use their own philosophies to understand and to create stock-related information, especially with the help of information and communication technologies (ICTs). Therefore, to understand risk communication in China, we must first comprehend not only what the government and the experts say, but also how investors make sense of what is said. As a result, this chapter attempts to answer the following two questions first: What communication practices do investors follow during the stock investment process? And what types of information concerns them?

Despite their many differences, small investors and big bankers share one thing in common. When asked, "What do you usually do when investing in securities," the majority describe a *process* with a start, progress, and an end. Constituted within this process are a cluster of communication practices that convey different types of information, aiming to transform uncertainties into securities. Anything but random, these practices are quite organized, as evidenced by the fact that investors use ordinal numbers (first, second) and prepositions (before, after) in expressions of time. Mr. Gao, a senior financial analyst and stock commentator, describes how this communication process typically works in its ideal form:

> The basis of stock investment is to get relevant information. So, first of all, in every stock investment, I always need to obtain the relevant information [obtaining information]. After that, I analyse it professionally in order to make sense of the data [making sense of information] (...) Sometimes, I discuss my views of the stocks with my friends ["sharing information" and "obtaining information"].

Finally, I buy or sell the stocks [trading order]. (...) People consult me about my analysis of the stocks from time to time [sharing information].[1]

From Gao's description, we can code four major clusters of communication practices based upon the reasoning process when investing in stocks: obtaining stock information (huoquxiaoxi in Chinese), making sense of information (lijiexiaoxi), trading stocks (jiaoyigupiao), and sharing stock information (jiaoliuxiaoxi). These communication practice categories are patterned in the sense that they occur repeatedly ("in every stock investment" from Gao). The first three clusters of communication practices relate more closely to the time order or logical reasoning. Both big bankers and small investors agree that every stock investment starts with the obtaining of stock-related information. They use the term "basis" to describe what obtaining stock information means to them in terms of stock investment. As Mr. Chen, a big investor puts it, "Without obtaining information, I can't do any trading." In other words, this cluster of practices forms the prerequisites (Shove, Pantzar, & Watson, 2012) for the following two steps, AKA the second and third clusters of practices: making sense of information and trading stocks.

Unlike the first three clusters of practices, the fourth category of communication practice, sharing stock information, represents a loose and flexible practice in the investment process. Not only Mr. Gao but many other investors mentioned that the time frame for sharing stock information is unfixed, completely dependent upon the situation. Though it seems not to be a compulsory step, it appears in the stock investors' communication process repeatedly. For the investors, sharing stock information is a special gesture, a signal based upon mutual understanding and extending far beyond delivering messages. It appears to be an act of giving, but in its nature, it asks for taking. This cluster of practices is fascinating because it represents a crucial aspect of how investors produce meaningful *guanxi* in the risk community of finance. The readers will see more about how this cluster of practices works in the following sections of the book.

Ideally, investors would like to follow a step-by-step investing process for obtaining information in order to make sense of the data obtained and to better trade stocks. This should grant them the sense of securities. However, they sometimes face difficulties and have to make changes during such process. When describing the interconnections (Shove et al., 2012) between different clusters of communication practices, a fifth cluster of communication practice emerges from the data, one that links one cluster of practices to another, coded as "evaluating practice." The evaluating practice serves to direct investors to engage in the other clusters of communication practices. Throughout the communication process of stock investment, the investors use various criteria to ascertain the effectiveness of their former communication practice; such communication practices have been observed in other practice theory as well (e.g. Craig, 2006).

Such observations may be shifting the stereotype of individual investors as a group of blind-minded, irrational, and desire-for-risk amateurs. Indeed, such investors systematically set up procedures and schedules, trying to understand the market using different communication practices. Every step taken by these investors focuses on security instead of uncertainty. And when they fail, they evaluate the previous practice poorly and shift to other practices in order to gain security in investment again. I code such situations as "practice-shifting moments." Most commonly, instead of rushing to trade stocks, investors re-obtain stock information because they could not successfully make sense of the information. For instance, Ms. Li, a retired worker, told me,

> The (stock) prices fluctuated so much this morning [obtaining information], but I cannot figure out why [evaluating the practice of 'making sense of information' as unsatisfactory]. (...) Therefore, I have to make a phone call to Teacher Wang to ask for his opinion [obtaining information].

Ms. Li's use of the term "therefore" (suoyi in Chinese) indicates the causal relationship between her unsatisfactory sensemaking of the information and her shift to the practice of obtaining another type of information. When such practice-shifting moments appear, the investors are dragged reluctantly from their planned ideal communication process, feeling uncertainty or even anxiety. They will try different strategies and reevaluate repeatedly until they feel secure about the information at hand and ready to move into the next step of the stock investment process. During this period, they depend highly on their *guanxi*, producing and enhancing a hierarchical relationship in risk communication between the "student" and "teacher," a topic discussed further in Chapter 6. Evaluation practices emerge not only in the midst of the investment process but also at its conclusion. For instance, almost all of the investors reported that they seek to obtain stock price information after trading to "see if my trading was smart or not" (from Ms. Yu, a financial expert now working for several consultant companies). This follow-up may reopen another stock investment process. Notably, the investors evaluate not only their own practice but also the practices of others.

Of course, each cluster of practices mentioned above contains other practices, some of which overlap with those in other clusters. The cluster of obtaining information, for example, includes various practices such as watching TV, reading newspapers and reports, listening to the radio, surfing the Internet, and talking with other people in different forms.

Some of these practices are individual-oriented, like obtaining stock quotes (kanpan), consulting the news (xinwen), or reading stock commentary (guping). Such actions do not necessarily involve sharing or exchanging investment information with others. Other practices embrace interactions with more participants, such as stock talk (liaogupiao), which combines the practices of obtaining and sharing information. The in vivo coding indicates that the participants identify various stock talks such as talking on the phone (dianhualiaotian), talking at a public gathering (jujiliaotian), discussing at an "elite club" (neibujuhui), talking at a family gathering (jiatingjuhui), or participating in an online group or forum (qunliao). In these different stock talks, the investors are either information seekers, sharers, or exchangers. The investors use informal stock talks to communicate information about stock opinions and insider information.

Among these varied practices, one can argue that digital technologies have become an important part of investors' communication process in recent years, enabling different types of practices such as online chatting or using stock software. But even this argument may underestimate or take for granted the influence of ICTs on the financial markets, an influence that can be traced to the beginning of the stock markets in the People's Republic of China. Without ICTs, the stage of financial risk would differ completely today: The majority of grassroots investors would be excluded from communication regarding stock-relevant information. On the other hand, it would be tech-centric to assert that ICTs are responsible for all the changes. Indeed, the power dynamics in risk communication for China's financial markets result from complex factors, from voluntary collusion between interest groups to a cultural and political background rooted in the society itself. This complex situation has catalyzed the revolution and distribution of ICTs in the stock investment communication process; meanwhile, these digital technologies impact the markets, bringing about a unique culture of risk, equality, and security.

To further approach the role that ICTs play within such contexts, we have to deconstruct people's stock investment communication practices. Looking at the data, I have found that the varied information being conveyed through the practices holds very different meanings for the investors who identify six primary types of stock investment information: stock quotes (gujia), trading orders (jiaoyixinxi), company information (gongsi xiaoxi), stock commentary (guping), stock opinions (kanfa), and insider information (neimuxiaoxi). Some project participants also communicate international news (guojixinwen) as important reference.

Different types of above information are interrelated. For instance, investors sometimes will obtain stock quote information and news first; they then make sense of this information in order to transform it into stock opinions or stock commentary. In order to complete the entire stock investment communication process successfully, investors use a variety of practices to convey information, thus attaching different meanings to the information itself as well as to related ideas of risk and equality. In the following sections, I explore how these types of information are communicated as well as the roles of ICTs in the process.

Stock Quotes and Trading Orders

A complete communication process in investment usually begins with the obtaining of stock quotes and ends with the sending out of trading orders. These two types of information hold a strong relationship: The trading orders may decide the stock prices, and the stock quotes may trigger different trading orders. Let's begin by discussing the communication of stock quotes first. Generally speaking, stock quotes form the very basis of investors' entire communication process, serving as a precondition for them to evaluate the risk and opportunities. Whether big or small, investors in China are extraordinarily picky and even "spoiled" when it comes to evaluating their practice and obtaining stock quote information. They require not only instant stock prices but also all data related to such securities' price performance, from recent trading volumes, price history, highest and lowest prices of the period, to the all-important indicators like the stochastic oscillator. These investors want to obtain accurate information quickly, with a clear presentation in graphs and charts; above all, they want this information to be free of cost.

Mr. Huang, a small investor, used to stay abroad for long periods of time while visiting his son. He had this to say about his experience of obtaining stock quotes there:

> You know what is strange about that place? Once I asked (my son) to have a look at the stock quote of Stock A in that local market. He looked through his online banking system, and told me that they provide the instant price (of Stock A) only—You need to pay to know more details! They (the bank) dared to ask for money! Can you imagine the same thing happening in China? Graphs, numbers, everything is (free) here.

While providing this anecdote, Mr. Huang showed me some evidence on his cell phone App. On the screen, there was a K-line graph and the simple moving average (SMA) of Stock A, which Huang had favorited. Mr. Huang and millions of Chinese investors take it for granted that they should obtain complimentary stock quotes and relevant information easily and swiftly, using the stock software or other communication technologies at hand. Of course, one must not overlook the fact that they may have paid for it already in one way or another, for instance, in the form commissions to the securities brokerages providing stock quotes and trading services. Overall, however, the commission rates are very low (usually around 0.025%, and sometimes even down to 0.012%)[2] and not related to the communication practices of obtaining stock quotes directly. Moreover, people also can obtain decent stock price data free of cost from various open websites, software, and well-distributed Apps. Indeed, some Chinese web portals even provide outside stock information freely, so much so that the Hong Kong Stock Exchange has to block them in order to ensure their business in selling stock quotes.[3] In brief, it is not an overstatement to say that stock quote information in China is communicated in a comparatively swift, open, and egalitarian way today.

But was this the case back in the 1990s, when digital media technologies were quickly developing yet not widely distributed in China? To respond to this question, we need to look closely at a particular communication practice for obtaining stock quotes, namely, *kanpan*. In Chinese, *kan* means "to watch" and *pan* refers to a "bowl" or a "chessboard." No reputable source has indicated why people call the stock markets a bowl. The investors assure me that they usually use *dapan* (big bowl in Chinese) as a metaphor to represent the stock quotes and indexes of the Shanghai Stock Exchange (SSE) and Shenzhen Stock Exchange (SZSE) in general. Meanwhile, they use dapangu (big-bowl securities) to indicate the important blue chips most influential to the market. Perhaps investors consider the market to be a bowl containing different securities with changing stock quotes—or, perhaps, it is just a chessboard upon which there are various pieces in movement.

More than any other, *kan* seems to be a trivial communication practice, meaning only to watch "the big bowl." But, it indeed sheds some light on the ways that people communicated stock quotes in the 1990s. First of all, *kan* means simply to watch or read the securities prices of "the big bowl," indicating that, even at the beginning of China's stock market, digital technology was mature enough to provide straightforward stock quotes instead of telegraphic codes to be interpreted. To compare, we can have a look at the term that English-speaking investors use to describe a practice similar to *kanpan*: tape reading. Before the development of the Internet and computer technology, many stock markets provided stock quotes and other relevant data through the so-called ticker tapes printed by ticker tape machines (Scantlin, 1963, 1966; Kavesh, Garbade, & Silber, 1978). The production of ticker tapes depended on the communication technology of printing telegraphy, and specific tape readers were required for interpreting and representing the ticker tapes (Preda, 2006; Sandvig, 2008). The clerks or so-called runners and board boys (Smitten, 2001; Nassar, 2004) then would update the price for the traders and brokers on the chalkboards. Though our communication technologies have evolved a great deal, the communication practices of the early years have left some permanent marks. It is said that the New York Stock Exchange's nickname, "the Big Board," may come from the practice of delivering stock quotations on chalkboards (Hashemian, 2001). Meanwhile, investors continue to use the term "tape reading" to refer to the practice of obtaining and making sense of prices and relevant information, even though the ticker tapes have long been replaced by computer networks.

Collard's (1974) *Chalk to Computers* documents the history of the stock exchange in Montreal. The title itself wonderfully captures the transformation of communication stock quotes not only in Canada but also in stock markets across North America and Europe. In China, to be fair, the history of *kanpan* indeed followed chalk to computers as well. But to the pride of the Chinese government authorities, such change only took a few years, and the Chalk Period occurred before the official opening of the two stock exchanges. The period was so short that it left no mark on investors' understanding of *kanpan*. From the beginning of the stock exchange in the 1990s, the once communist society embraced the technological revolution, meaning that ticker tapes would never be used in the People's Republic of China.

With ICTs, stock quotes could be delivered straightforwardly for people to *kan* (watch); it was much faster and more convenient than in the past.[4] Despite its advantages, the communication process was not terribly satisfactory during the market's early stages. Yes, digital technologies were being applied and used, but only by a few institutions. The limited distribution of ICTs constrained the power of which in facilitating the communication of stock quotes. Mr. Chen, a millionaire investor, was a penniless new university graduate back then; all he had was 2,000 Chinese Yuan borrowed from his father. He characterized his impression of kanpan with two terms: crowd and chaotic.

> It was summer. I started to test the water (of the market). Many people were there in the stock exchange hall. The mass was a mess. Everyone was sweating like hell...There was only one computer in the hall showing the stock quotes. You had to be strong enough to get a better position to even see the data on the screen.

Two other big investors with a similarly long experience in the stock market, Mr. Gao and Ms. Yu, confirm what Mr. Chen has described, that the assessment of ICTs was extremely rare and the evaluation of obtaining stock quotes was always low. Both Mr. Gao and Ms. Yu are professional experts in finance and provided me with insights regarding risk communication at the beginning of this chapter. According to the investors, the criteria for the communication practice of *kanpan* are very simple: speed, accuracy, convenience, and detail. None of these criteria were satisfied at that time. Ms. Yu described the difficulties of *kanpan* in the early days:

> You could not get instant and accurate prices, let alone the price histories or other indicators of stocks and graphs for analysis...What I was saying was not the worst situation. Considering that there were not many securities brokerages in Shanghai, some people could not reach the instant stock quotes at all.

The number of securities brokerages was limited, and there were few electronic stock quotation boards. Local citizens swarmed to the limited boards to *kanpan*, causing serious bottlenecks. The uncertainties of obtaining stock quotes accurately and quickly were so high that the practice of *kanpan* itself became a major risk in the communication process, equally for almost all investors.

The major players of risk communication soon stepped into this anarchic situation, though with very different intentions. The government authorities, positioning themselves as the game rulers and risk managers, certainly wanted to control the uncertainties of financial communication. Meanwhile, they also needed to fulfill the Communist Party's promise to Chinese society to "serve the people." This promise formed the foundation of the party's ideology throughout the reign of Chairman Mao, and it continues to the present (Zhang, 2002; Nolan, 2005; Wilsdon, 2007). Once upon a time, "the people" were greatly drawn to capitalism; clearly, they had had enough of the impoverished conditions that were ubiquitous during the closed-door period.[5] They sent out a clear message by gathering together in crowds in stock exchange halls and near stock quotation boards: We want money, and we want stocks. How could they invest in stocks without quick access to stock quotes? It seems only natural that the government authorities would respond to this public call, enhancing the communication process to create active and energetic markets for the public.

But did they have to do respond? By handing over stock quotes to the public, the government handed over the right of financial investment— as well as the risk—to individuals. The Chinese government also could have chosen simply to develop a small-scale ICT platform only for the professional institutions to *kanpan*, thus letting experts deal with the uncertainties in the financial system. There may be a political and cultural reason that the Chinese government chose a grand and chaotic market over a small and professional one: The social atmosphere in China back then still stuck to hardcore socialism. From a socialist perspective, it would be difficult to allow a professional-oriented risk culture in which the majority trusts the elite minority to deal with financial risk. Following a "more the merrier" strategy, government authorities sought a political breakthrough, especially those in Shanghai and Shenzhen. At the beginning of the 1990s, the People's Bank of China, with conservative attitudes and great caution, applied a so-called membership mechanism in finance, allowing only the local financial institutions to be members of the stock exchanges. This mechanism excluded nonlocal institutions and investors from the game. In an open interview by the Sina Web portal, Xu Shimin,[6] one of the earliest experts working for the SSE, discussed the negotiation with political leaders at the Bank, noting that some nonlocal brokerages were able to become members of the SSE. Not long after, the Bank loosed the constraints, and both the SSE and SZSE could recruit nonlocal institutions as members.

In essence, the number of potential investors expanded largely, but this political breakthrough alone was insufficient to reduce the risk of *kanpan*. Without an effective way to broadcast stock quotes to the masses, neither the local nor the nonlocal financial institutions were able to attract more investments. Both stock exchanges then sought the help of communication technology, soon updating the computer system while conducting the data network through satellites, ensuring that instant stock quotes could reach both the local and nonlocal brokerages almost simultaneously (Ma, 2003). According to Xu, the SSE even asked the local engineering institution to invent a specific radio station to communicate stock quotes for small investors.

Meanwhile, the capital felt the chance in risk like a shark sensing blood in the water. Pagers, cellular phones, telephone hotlines, televisions, newspapers, magazines: Both state-owned and private enterprises scrambled to provide instant stock quotes services through these various communication platforms. Some of these platforms gained popularity in the 1990s and early 2000s only because they could deliver stock quotes. Specific attention had to be paid to the inner differences between these technologies in the pre-mobile phone and pre-personal computer era. For mass media, the major communication form was unidirectional. Similar to watching the stock quotation boards, the people using televisions, radios, newspapers, and magazines for *kanpan* were all passive receivers of stock quote information. Their communicative positions included being readers, watchers, and listeners—totally dependent on the mass communicator to broadcast information. The investors were still not able to obtain the exact data they wanted immediately and swiftly; they had to wait for the release of information from the media's end. Regarding pagers (the so-called BP machine in China) and telephone hotlines, the situation differed. Investors became more active, sending out messages or making phone calls to obtain the exact stock quotes they desired. The public's overall evaluation of *kanpan* was still rather unsatisfactory, but some of the criteria of *kanpan* practice, such as speediness, accuracy, and convenience, were partially satisfied with the development of ICT. Another important change was that people started to position themselves as users of *kanpan* instead of merely watchers. They became more engaged in the process of financial communication for stock prices.

But what really transformed investors into active users in *kanpan* was the arrival of personal computers and stock software. The major initiator of this communication revolution was not government authority, but another important player in risk communication—the brokerages. While the government and the media outlets aimed to increase egalitarianism for stock quotes, the brokerages sensed an opportunity to build a solid wall between the stock-quote haves and have-nots. The dawning of this realization by brokerages might have happened by chance. A famous individual investor nicknamed Billionaire Yang was one of few wealthy people when the SSE opened. He was once a worker with almost no educational background in finance, but by that time, he already had earned his first pot of gold from government bonds. On the same day as the official opening of the SSE, Yang declared that his volume of trade equaled half of the entire market volume.

> Because of my influence on the market, the brokerage Shenyin Securities set up a 'big investor room' only for me. (They) did not dare to call it Big Investor Room back then; instead they used the term 'Customer Service Room.'[7]

The cautious attitude of the brokerages was reasonable, because they did not want to be perceived as hostile to socialism and the egalitarian culture of Chinese society. However, this attitude was soon replaced by the desire to attract more big investors to their brokerages. More big investors meant more commissions and other service fees, and it also meant that the brokerages could dig for gold from investors' margin trading. Almost all of the big brokerages opened a VIP room, or as coded in vivo, a "big investor room" for wealthy investors. Later, they also opened the so-called "middle investor room" for less wealthy ones. These big and middle investors could enjoy all of the limited ICT resources to *kanpan*, including personal computers, the Internet, and stock software. In addition, they enjoyed air-conditioning, a free pager service, and sometimes even free meals and snacks. While the crowd and the once penniless Mr. Chen were sweating in the big stock exchange hall, struggling to see the stock quotes, Billionaire Yang stayed cool in air-conditioned VIP rooms, watching computers to obtain instant information about the market. In this way, the brokerages made large profits while reducing uncertainties in *kanpan* for a wealthy minority, instead of equally serving "the people" like the government.

After several years of investing, Mr. Chen eventually obtained permission to enter the Big Investor Room. He told me about that day with a bit of gloating, clearly content with the fact that he was able to actively use computers while others were mere watchers in *kanpan*:

> The small investors had to stay in the stock exchange hall and watch the stock quotation board, but we big investors could use computers—usually everyone had one computer—in the Big Investor Room to check the stock prices and other data.

These computers usually were equipped with stock software, brought to mainland China by Taiwanese companies (Xie, 2003). One of the most famous and popular software was Qianlong (Zhuang, Hu, & Ye, 2008; Hu et al., 2015), and today's stock software in China is believed to use it as a model. Using stock software, big investors can quickly locate the exact stock quotes they want, with very detailed graphs and charts showing important indicators. Time also was compressed by this new technology, and users could easily track down the price history of securities, while watchers could only access instant (and not-so-instant) stock quotes.

As if this gap were not enough, the people in the Big Investor Room enjoyed another privilege in communication: They could send out their trading orders with priority service. Ironically, this privilege is only possible due to the specific trading system in China's financial market. Since the official launch of China's stock market, ICTs have been rooted in its trading system. It is important to point out that the SZSE used a system of open outcry once upon a time, but shortly after, they began applying an electronic system for order matching. Meanwhile, the SSE facilitated electronic order matching from the very beginning. According to Xu Shimin's memory, the SSE thought about using the open outcry system before, because "it makes a teeming crowd, and it is commonly used." But the training session did not go well, because the trader being trained made several mistakes. The risk seemed too high, and Wei Wenyuan, a former executive at the SSE, decided to make up an electronic trading system, which later was built with the cooperation of a university research associate named Xie Wei,[8] along with several other experts. Xie majored in mathematics and worked in the Information Department at that time; later, he became the vice general manager of the SSE. The trading system of the stock market was based upon three steps: First, the investors buy and sell orders that were recorded by the counter clerks in brokerages. Then, those clerks would make phone calls to the so-called authorized clerks of the brokerage in the stock exchange. Finally, the authorized clerks would input the orders in the electronic system using computers, and the digital system would be run to match the orders.

Compared to the nonelectronic system, the auctions of China's 1990s stock markets were much faster, convenient, and accurate. The government's original intention was to ensure that the system would "serve the people." Wei Wenyuan even rented a huge square in Shanghai to make certain that the large number of citizens could be served by the counter clerks outside of the brokerages there. But again, the brokerages were seeking to profit from serving the minority. Back in the 1990s, it was common to see small investors crowded into the big exchange hall of a stock brokerage, waiting in long queues in front of one counter to do their trading. Their only hope was that by the time they made it to the clerk and handed in the form with trading information, the stock prices would not change too much, making their order void. Simultaneously, the brokerages provided clerks and telephone lines just for investors in the Big Investor Room, seeking to make their experience in the communication practice of trading as pleasant as possible. By satisfying big investors in kanpan and trading, the brokerages encouraged these wealthy individuals to trade stocks more frequently; thus, they could gain more commissions. At that time, they themselves might not have considered the impacts of these conditions, the excessive speculation running rampant then and continuing until now.

In general, during this particular phase in history, ICTs were limited to priority groups, and inequalities in risk distribution were established through the communication practices of *kanpan* and trading. Small investors with no ICT access faced the majority of uncertainties. The question is: what does this risk hierarchy in *kanpan* mean for both sides of the playing field? Mr. Chen's comments may shed some light on this issue: "Back then, I knew the prices changed a bit quicker than other people. I reacted faster, and it gave me a big advantage because of the information asymmetry." Big investors were clearly satisfied with this system, and took advantage of the asymmetry in *kanpan* and trading. Their sense of security at that time did not rely only on their own access to ICTs, but also on the fact that others were kept away from the communication technologies. At the same time, small investors were fiercely complaining to the government that "the brokerages only care about the big investors." This situation left room for the rich ones to manipulate the market, with public uncertainty serving as a weapon. When one person's security is based on another's risk, a zero-sum risk culture has been created. This risk culture began with the physical and technological separation between the small investors in halls and big investors in VIP rooms. The excessive speculation further increased the tensions, adding fuel to the fire, to the point that the big investors were eventually called "bankers." They were not born manipulators of risk. They became ones due to the unequal communication of information.

During this stage, it seems that it was the money that mattered the most. The wealthiest individuals were the information (stock quotes) haves, and the poor ones were the have-nots facing risk. The so-called public information was not genuinely public, the one unexpected result of which was the increase in stock quote value. Expertise did not matter as much under such circumstances. Mr. Gao, who has had decent training from a college of financial investment, found that it was even not necessary to apply expertise to make sense of the stock quotes.

> You certainly still needed some basic concepts about the market and the stocks. But overall, at that time, with the instant and historic stock prices and ask/bid queue only—and maybe some national news for reference, you could do the trading from a much better position than the small investors.

Devaluing of Stock Quotes

Mr. Huang, a small investor, was full of envy and curiosity about the VIP rooms and ICT facilities for *kanpan*, but surpassing the gap between the bankers and small investors was not easy. The practice of "sharing stock quotes" may have helped; the information have-mores shared the stock quotes with the have-nots and have-lesses. But such practices required solid *guanxi* (relationships). For example, Mr. Huang once asked one friend to take him to the Big Investor Room to "have a look at it." This was a "practice-shifting moment" for Mr. Huang, showing how uncertain he'd become about obtaining stock quotes and trading decently. His experience afterward illustrates how the priority groups carefully protected their privileges in *kanpan* and trading. Huang said,

> They (the big investors) staying in the room seemed to know each other there. The staff in the brokerages knew them all as well, and they served them only. It was just…meaningless to stay there. I felt that I was looked down upon. They looked at you like a stranger. I did know a small investor scrounging free meals in the Middle Investor Room. He was chucked out of the room by the brokerage. Embarrassing.

After telling this story, he shrugged. "Well, who knows? Nowadays the stock software is everywhere. Things are precious when they are rare, I guess."

According to the World Bank, 1.78% of the Chinese population had access to the Internet using different ICTs in 2000. By 2016, that percentage had increased to over 50%.[9] The dramatic spread of personal computers and mobile phones seems to have transformed communication about stock quotes, thus changing people's everyday routines. Most visibly, ICTs have freed investors from a particular physical space, which in the 1990s included big-city brokerages. At that time, people had to go to either the exchange halls or the VIP rooms to obtain instant stock quotes before trading. Like the majority of financial markets in the world, China's stock market opened and closed during typical working hours on weekdays: from 9:15 am to 11:30 am and from 1:00 pm to 3:00 pm, with a lunch break between. After 9:30 am, the changing stock prices and relevant data were released continually, unless the securities were suspended. Thus, if the investors wanted a satisfactory *kanpan* practice, they had to stay in the halls or VIP rooms, keeping an eye on the market from time to time. Mr. Chen, a big investor who graduated from a top university in Shanghai, had a decent offer from a large company when entering the stock market. He was so attracted to financial trading that he had to turn down the offer. Talking about this decision, he still seems very torn, as if he had traveled back to the 1990s.

He remembered wistfully the moment when he stepped into the office and told the recruiting team that he would not accept their offer.

> It (the job offer) was a very good chance. Some of my classmates continued their path in academia, and are now working as faculty at top universities in the US. Some went to the big banks or companies…They are very successful people now. I chose to be a (full-time) investor, and kid you not, I did a good job, too. But if I have had a second chance? I really don't know.

Many Chinese people made the same choice as Chen's classmates at that time, simply because their daily routines could not incorporate the communication practices of *kanpan*. Xia, the now college student who sneakily used a smartphone to trade stocks during class in Chapter 1, does not have to make the choice between having a job and being an investor. Xia said,

> My mum would literally faint if I became a freelancer (of stock investment). No way. Work for a fund or a brokerage or a bank, fine. But do it as an individual? No, no, no. What shall I say to the mother of my girlfriend? 'Auntie, I want to marry your daughter. I have no full-time job, my job is to stay at home doing stock investment?' I will work for a company while continuing to trade stocks. No conflicts at all.

Another metamorphosis that ICTs have catalyzed is the breakdown of risk hierarchies between the Big Investor Room/Small Investor Hall mechanism. While the Big Investor Room promised security in *kanpan*, the Small Investor Hall was full of uncertainties. As Mr. Huang has said, the things once held precious are definitely not so precious anymore. A wealthy minority no longer controls the situation. Walking into an ordinary stock exchange hall in Shanghai, I saw rows of computers in the big room, free for investors to use, plus a big electronic stock quotation board on the wall. Even the elder people, usually regarded as laggards (Rogers, 2002) in terms of technology distribution, fluently used the machines for *kanpan* and trading. When they wanted to talk with each other while partaking in *kanpan*, they would take a seat in front of the big electronic board and sit there. Among those investors, the strictly non-ICT users, like Ms. Li and Mr. Qian, seem to be an absolute minority. Both of them basically rely on the electronic stock quotation board to obtain stock quotes, and they use the phone or go to the counter to buy and sell stocks. Sitting beside Ms. Li in the stock exchange hall, I asked her to describe what she was doing and how she felt:

> I am watching the numbers changing on the board. I have to wait until the data I want show up on the board. The feeling of delay is

not good, but I have gotten used to that. The data shown on the board were quite limited. Those people who use computers can locate (the data) much quicker and react sooner than me, and I am afraid I might be slow in reacting…But, I don't want to learn the new techniques, because watching the board is my habit.

Clearly, Ms. Li's evaluation of *kanpan* is low. More importantly, her high evaluation of ICT users' practices and low evaluation of non-ICT users' practices create a sense of inequality, which she associates with the concept of risk. In the previous period, when new media technologies were not so distributed, an adversarial *kanpan* relationship occurred between the big investors and the small ones. With the dawning of the digital media era, a competitive relationship still exists, but between the ICT users and non-ICT "watchers." If access is not the problem, what prevents people like Ms. Li and Mr. Qian from using ICTs? Is digital media technology like stock software too difficult to use? Both Li and Qian denied this idea, saying ICT devices do not require "very much expertise," noting that they are comparatively easy to learn if one desires to do so. Ms. Li insisted that it is just a personal choice and habit; she prefers to stick to watching the big board for stock quotes. Mr. Qian is more open, saying that his grandson plans to teach him how to use a computer: "I believe that I can use a computer in the future to do kanpan," said Qian, "Besides, when I really need some information about the stock prices, I ask my friends in the hall for a favour."

But how big is such a favor? Let's compare it with the "favor" that Mr. Huang asked of his friend when he requested to be taken to the Big Investor Room back in the 1990s. Like Mr. Huang, Mr. Qian also experienced a "practice-shifting moment" due to the lack of ICT use. He was so unsatisfied with his own *kanpan* practice that he turned to ICT users for help. They both relied on a sort of guanxi (relationship) during this moment, a human connection that, in their words, is friendship. The difference between these scenarios is that Mr. Huang's experience was a one-time scenario, and he felt uneasy, indicating that it was a rather large favor to ask. By contrast, Mr. Qian's favor seems to be fairly casual and occurs on a daily basis. This difference also is confirmed by ICT users who share stock quotes, Mr. Huang, Ms. Lin, and Mr. Ma. Mr. Huang, a small investor with whom the reader might already be familiar, casually handed his mobile phone to a person nearby for *kanpan* during one of our interviews. Ms. Lin, a small investor in her fifties, called the practice of sharing stock quotes "a little favor":

We help each other when needed. It (sharing stock quotes with others) is easy, you know. It does not cost me much time or effort. The stock prices are not difficult to obtain. I just pass the exact information on to them (the inquirers) without thinking.

From Lin's statement, we can make several observations. First, the sense of security attached to *kanpan* has become more equal today thanks to ICTs; ironically, however, this security devalues stock quotes as information. When she says that she delivers the stock quotes "without thinking," Lin indicates that she perceives stock prices as "raw" information, meaning they have yet to be made sense of. According to Mr. Gao, the practice of making sense of stock quotes was easier for ICT owners (i.e., big investors in the 1990s). Due to the information asymmetry, big investors could simply use the time lapses to conduct trading, even without professionally analyzing the stock quotes. However, since the disappearance of information asymmetry in *kanpan*, it has become impossible for big investors like Chen and Gao to gain money merely by taking advantage of other people's risk. They can no longer lag behind, putting little effort into making sense of the stock quotes. Their security based upon other's risk has dissolved. But small investors, new users of ICT, also face a dilemma. With the equal communication of stock quotes, such information is not as valuable as it was before. Small investors have found that they can do little with the raw information only.

Though the stock quotes have become somewhat devalued in people's perceptions, exchanging "small information" and doing each other "little favors" means a great deal to the small investors. According to investors, sharing stock quotes is not necessarily connected to people's practices of stock investment, nor is it a contractual obligation. Instead, it is a voluntary practice controlled by the sharer. To share could mean providing something that others lack, locating oneself at a higher, positive, and decent social position, and generating a self-image of being helpful and friendly. In the case of requiring and sharing stock quotes, people have the mutual understanding that such a favor is small and will be returned in the form of another small favor. In Ms. Lin's words, "We help each other when needed." The small investors constructed equal bonds with others in the sense that their positions are perceived as reversible, and thus produce a feeling of security based upon a sense of friendship and community. This community is very appealing to small investors, so much so that many small investors still go to the stock exchange halls even though ICTs have released people from the physical constraints of *kanpan* and trading for years. The daily exchange of raw information as a little favor has become an important part of social life, creating and reinforcing equal relations within the community. When exchanging information, the small investors construct cooperative relations instead of "zero-sum relations," meaning they help each other for the mutual good.

But this situation raises even more questions: Why is the community predominantly composed of small investors? Why are the big investors the "others" instead of "us"? Mr. Kang, another small investor, also used the term "we" to refer to the small investors only, with a bit more radical stance.

I am relaxed when talking to other small investors, because we are all small investors. We are small potatoes...Why should a banker share information with us? We can provide him nothing. The small investors should help each other because we are weaker than the big investors in many ways. If we are united, we can increase our risk resistance capacity.

There is some truth in Kang's statements; theoretically, if the small investors "unite," they can conquer the big investors, individuals or institutions, with no question. But the small investors are too scattered. With thousands of listed companies on the market and an information explosion, it would be impossible for them to make sense of the stock quotes and estimate the risk in a united and consistent manner. What they are doing seems to be trivial. However, that day-to-day exchange of not-so-valuable information produces a sense of security by at least having an equal starting point as the big investors. Meanwhile, "by having each other's backs," they produce a sense of security through equal and friendly interpersonal relations. But what if they want to obtain more valuable information, asking for a "big favor" instead of a small one? What if the information inquirer does not have equally valuable information to exchange with the information sharer? A hierarchical relationship regarding such communication then is produced, with the sharer's position on top and the uncertain inquirer's position below.

In the 1990s, when stepping into the Big Investor Room, Mr. Huang felt that he was a complete stranger. He was being "looked down upon" by the people there. Twenty years later, Mr. Kang had similar feelings when he faced big investors, to the extent he'd rather stay with the members of the small investor club. The separation of physical places in the 1990s eventually placed the investors in unequal social spaces (Bourdieu, 1985; Witteborn, 2011), different networks of financial communication. There can be no doubt that the public distribution of ICTs has torn down the risk hierarchies in *kanpan* and trading in a dramatic way; however, before celebrating the digital media era, we need to pay attention to the new, "digital" risk in *kanpan* that has emerged. Majority of interviewees complained that they have suffered at least one experience of technological breakdown in relation to stock investing software. The small investor Mr. Kang, for example, complained to me that two brokerages he knew provided "really terrible" service in supporting their software, that they did not update their software often enough, plus their servers breakdown for several times. Kang said to me,

The experiences (with those software services provided) were so terrible, to the point that I have to open account in a third brokerage firm, just because when the two other servers are out of work again, I can have another backup.

Xia, a college student, said to me that the unstable Internet access was also a problem.

> I was just about to buy in a stock that I have observed for two weeks, and I thought it was about the right time, that a bull market was waiting head. You guess what? Our campus Internet was slow as hell that day. When I finally logged in my account, it was too late. The bankers has already started their game.

In such instances, the small investors' *kanpan* practices were not smooth, and their trading orders could not be sent properly. But all in all, these uncertainties are random and do not happen on a daily basis as they did back in the 1990s for China's small investors. Moreover, such mechanical risks are also equal for all investors. In Chapter 1, we saw a typical case: The big brokerage firm Everbright suffered a major technical error in its communication of trading orders. The big investor Mr. Gao told me that one finance company he used to work for encountered a power failure once, that the traders and analysts from the whole building were at lost, staring at their computer with black screens blankly. "To be frankly, it was a hilarious moment," Gao said to me, "but my former boss's face turned green. That crisis caused him a fortune, of course."

To conclude this chapter, one small investor, Mr. Qin, used a metaphor to comment on the new dynamics brought about by ICTs. He referred to the whole communication process of financial investment as a racing game: "This (*kanpan* and trading) is the very basic starting line of stock investment. I am glad that I have not been delayed." But overall, a starting line is just a starting line, and even equipped by ICTs, some small investors still feel that they are the underdogs of risk distribution while others have the upper hand. To understand them, we need to look at what happens between the starting gun and the finish line, which I will further discuss in the next chapter.

Notes

1 I use line-by-line coding (Strauss & Corbin, 1998; Charmaz, 2006) as the analysis method in dealing with the data. Particularly, I use the technique of in vivo coding to generate crucial concepts in this study. In vivo coding means that the concepts are identified and named based on the participants' own words (Glaser & Strauss, 1967; Strauss & Corbin, 1998; Charmaz, 2006). This method is especially useful because this study takes place in China and targets China's investors who have their own terms to define stock investment, communicative practices, risk, and other relevant issues.

2 See http://stock.jrj.com.cn/2017/11/24015623687987.shtml

3 The price for stock quotes provided by the Hong Kong Stock Exchange can be viewed here: www.hkex.com.hk/eng/prod/dataprod/la/prices/Fee_Schedule.htm

4 One thing for sure is that ticker taping and the printing telegraph were once new digital technologies for the Western market as well. It is also interesting to look at the power dynamics in financial communication before and after the adoption of such techniques during that period.
5 See the studies of Shapiro (2001), Almond et al. (2007), and Cheng and Zhan (2018) for more detail.
6 See "Twenty Years of Memory" by Xu Shimin: http://finance.sina.com.cn/stock/stocktalk/20101217/08219121883.shtml
7 See the interview here: http://smgtv.eastday.com/d/20070821/u1a344276.html
8 See Wei Wenyuan's interview here: http://100.sufe.edu.cn/f6/75/c487a63093/page.htm
9 See https://data.worldbank.org/indicator/IT.NET.USER.ZS?locations=CN

References

Aitken, M. J., Berkman, H., & Mak, D. (2001). The use of undisclosed limit orders on the Australian Stock Exchange. *Journal of Banking & Finance*, 25(8), 1589–1603.

Almond, D., Edlund, L., Li, H., & Zhang, J. (2007). *Long-term effects of the 1959–1961 China famine: Mainland China and Hong Kong* (No. w13384). Cambridge, MA: National Bureau of Economic Research.

Bourdieu, P. (1985). The social space and the genesis of groups. *Theory and Society*, 14(6), 723–744.

Charmaz, K. (2006). *Constructing grounded theory: A practical guide through qualitative research*. London: Sage Publications.

Cheng, E., & Zhan, Z. (2018). A study of unnatural deaths during the difficult three year period in China, 1959–1961. *Science & Society*, 82(2), 171–202.

Collard, E. A. (1974). *Chalk to computers: The story of the Montreal Stock Exchange*. Quebec: Bibliothèque Nationale du Québec.

Craig, R. T. (2006). Communication as a practice. In G. J. Shepherd, J. St. John, & T. Striphas (Eds.) *Communication as …: Perspectives on theory* (pp. 38–47). Thousand Oaks, CA: Sage.

Glaser, B. G., & Strauss, A. (1967). *The discovery of grounded theory: Strategies for qualitative research*. Hawthorne, NY: Aldine de Gruyter.

Hashemian, R. V. (2001). *Financial markets for the rest of us: An easy guide to money, bonds, futures, stocks, options, and mutual funds*. San Jose, CA: Writers Club Press.

Hertz, E. (1998). *The trading crowd: An ethnography of the Shanghai stock market* (Vol. 108). Cambridge: Cambridge University Press.

Hu, Y., Zhang, X., Feng, B., Xie, K., & Liu, M. (2015). itrade: A mobile data-driven stock trading system with concept drift adaptation. *International Journal of Data Warehousing and Mining (IJDWM)*, 11(1), 66–83.

Kavesh, R. A., Garbade, K. D., & Silber, W. L. (1978). Technology, communication and the performance of financial markets: 1840–1975. *The Journal of Finance*, 33(3), 819–832.

Ma, Q. (Ed.). (2003). *The history of China's stock markets*. Beijing: Citic Publishing House.

Nassar, D. S. (2004). *How to get started in active trading and investing*. New York: McGraw-Hill Professional.

Nolan, P. H. (2005). China at the crossroads. *Journal of Chinese Economic and Business Studies*, 3(1), 1–22.

Preda, A. (2006). Socio-technical agency in financial markets: The case of the stock ticker. *Social Studies of Science*, 36(5), 753–782.

Rogers, E. M. (2002). Diffusion of preventive innovations. *Addictive Behaviors*, 27(6), 989–993.

Sandvig, C. (2008). *Wireless play and unexpected innovation. Digital youth, innovation, and the unexpected.* Cambridge, MA: The MIT Press.

Scantlin, J. R. (1963). *U.S. Patent No. 3,082,402.* Washington, DC: U.S. Patent and Trademark Office.

Scantlin, J. R. (1966). *U.S. Patent No. 3,249,919.* Washington, DC: U.S. Patent and Trademark Office.

Shapiro, J. (2001). *Mao's war against nature: Politics and the environment in revolutionary China.* Cambridge: Cambridge University Press.

Shove, E., Pantzar, M., & Watson, M. (2012). *The dynamics of social practice: Everyday life and how it changes.* London: Sage Publications.

Smitten, R. (2001). *Jesse Livermore: World's greatest stock trader.* New York: John Wiley & Sons.

Strauss, A., & Corbin, J. (1998). *Basics of qualitative research: Techniques and procedures for developing grounded theory*, 2nd ed. Thousand Oaks, CA: Sage Publications.

Wilsdon, J. (2007). China: The next science superpower? *Engineering & Technology*, 2(3), 28–31.

Witteborn, S. (2011). Constructing the forced migrant and the politics of space and place-making. *Journal of Communication*, 61(6), 1142–1160.

Xie, B. (Ed) (2003). *A global comparative study on stock markets.* Beijing: Tsinghua University Press.

Zhang, J. (2002). Will the government "serve the people"? The development of Chinese e-government. *New Media & Society*, 4(2), 163–184.

Zhuang, R., Hu, B., & Ye, Z. (2008). Minimal spanning tree for Shanghai-Shenzhen 300 stock index. In *Evolutionary Computation, 2008. CEC 2008. (IEEE World Congress on Computational Intelligence)* (pp. 1417–1424). IEEE.

4   Communicating National Affairs

As Chapter 3 discussed, the emergence of information and communication technologies (ICTs) in financial communication has broken down the old risk hierarchies in communicating stock quotes and trading orders in China. However, we also should pay attention to the fact that new inequalities have emerged in the changing landscape of financial communication. Quickly adapting to the new system, the bankers have found updated ways of taking advantage of the small investors. Mr. Chen, a big investor, showed me a "common trick" to manipulate the markets. He opened his stock trading software, located a particular security, and pointed out its order book[1] on the screen.

> You see? There is a huge number of sell orders hanging there. Do you think the bankers are gonna get away? Yes? Then you would be fooled. Such orders are just to terrify the small investors. The bankers want more securities from them, and they use this way of getting small investors to panic and sell off their stocks. If they really wanted to get out, why would they use limit orders[2] and set the selling point at a comparatively high price? It's also a warning to others banker that 'Hey, I am taking charge of this one. Stay away from it, guys.' It's funny to see, and it sometimes happens, that another strong banker steps in and 'eats' all the orders. It happened before, and I thought. 'Wow, the poor former banker must be angry as hell...' The same trick can be applied to a situation where a banker wants to sell out of a security as well. He just pretends to buy a huge amount of certain securities at a lower price, waits for the hot-headed small investors to join in, and bang, they cancel the former orders and sell out the securities at a higher price made by the sanhu.

These tricks introduced by Mr. Chen could only work in the digital age. In the early 1990s, the small investors could not even get stock quotes smoothly, let alone the intended trading orders recorded on the order books. Small investors may be enjoying a newly found security as a result of ICTs. They have become more certain about what's going on in the markets and with other investors. At the same time, they also are facing uncertainties they have never seen before: the underlying meaning of stock quotes and trading orders. Is it a green flag or a red one? Is a trap or an opportunity waiting ahead? Meanwhile, the bankers can be more certain of these questions because they can completely take charge of a security using their capital, gaining the upper hand once again in the sensemaking process of stock quotes and trading orders. The small investors then need to work out another way of dealing with the new risk. This chapter focuses on this sensemaking process, examining the role of ICTs.

Analyzing and Guessing

According to investors, stock quotes in the digital media era represent mere raw information instead of directional content. In essence, this information needs to be made sense of and generated into predictions before commencing with stock trading. It's a "cooking" process, a series of mediating practices linking different clusters of communication practices together. So what does this process look like? The big investor, Chen, points a finger to his computer in his study room and explains to me how he makes sense of the changing stock quotes:

> You can see from the stock price that it fluctuates because the investors with a long position (duotou) are struggling against the investors with a short position (kongtou). However, the stochastic oscillator indicates that the ones with a long position have become weak, so I think the price of this stock may go down soon. I will be prepared to sell it.

For Chen, stock quotes involve a competition between the investors with a long position (who buy the stocks in anticipation of the price increasing) and those with a short position (who sell the stocks in anticipation of the price decreasing). Therefore, stock prices are the natural consequence of buyers' and sellers' actions when trading stocks. When there are more investors buying than selling, the price of a certain stock increases, and vice versa. These investors use their capital flow to compete with each other, following the perspective that the long position's winning equals the short position's loss, indeed reinforcing the zero-sum culture of finance. The issue of risk emerges in the uncertainty regarding the next move of the market, portfolio, or listed company, leading to a sense of distrust in one's own predictions. The one to more accurately predict the next move of the market—or make better sense of the stock quotes—gains a better position in such zero-sum relations.

Theoretically, there is little room to take advantage of information asymmetry in *kanpan* and trading in the ICT era. As a result, expertise should be the most important factor differentiating the upper group from the lower group in financial risk. Most of the professional have-mores in my study, regardless of whether they are small or big investors, believe that expertise does make a difference. Ms. Yu, a senior financial analyst, obtained her Master's degree in finance from a top university in the United States. She invited me to her home and showed me a large shelf of books describing how to analyze stock prices. She made this statement:

> During my college days, I learned how to technically analyze the stock market. I continued to read books written by local analysts to learn how to systematically analyze the changes in stock prices... My skills have been tested and improved over years and years of analyzing stock prices. Thus, I can predict the investors' trading more accurately than those who do not have a professional background in finance.

Not only Ms. Yu but the majority of professional have-mores I interviewed attached importance to education, self-training, and experience. These credentials added to their expertise, positioning them as professional analyzers. These participants associate "accuracy" with the criterion they use to evaluate the practice of analyzing stock prices. After generating directional information from their analyses, some investors re-obtain the latest stock prices to see if their predictions were accurate. Their professional background in finance offers security to investors because such experience is associated with certainty in prediction accuracy. Ms. Yu mentioned that she explains and predicts the stock prices in a "systematic" way, relating her profession to the investors' patterns of thinking and doing when analyzing stock practices. Thus, the investors follow certain rules and theories that typically have been tested by their experiences and usually are associated with higher prediction accuracy.

Unlike inequality in ICT use, which is constructed as coverable and conquerable, the investors understand that inequality between investors' qualifications is difficult to reduce, requiring long-term professional training and practices. Mr. Zeng, a junior stock commentator and a small investor, says that it is "absolutely true" (tianjingdiyi) that professional investors who are have-mores tend to make better sense of stock prices. Zeng said, "Do you know how much effort I have put into gaining professional knowledge? Of course I can predict the stock prices more accurately than those who know nothing about the market." From this description, we again see that investors conceptualize an insurmountable distance between the professional have-mores and professional have-lesses, and based on this inequality, the professional have-mores produce a privileged position, generating more accurate directional information.

If, for the professional have-mores, the making sense of stock quotes is "analyzing", how is this cluster of practice perceived by the professional have-lesses? Unlike the variety seen in capital statues among the

professional have-mores, all of the professional have-lesses I have interviewed are small investors, except for one person. Once I stayed in a
stock exchange hall with Mr. Qian, who was busy watching the stock
quotes. I asked him if he was "analyzing the stock prices." He laughed.

> No, no, I am not analyzing. I am just blindly guessing what these
> stock prices really mean. I am not so sure. I have to take a risk by
> gambling. I hope I am lucky this time. Let's see. If it increases to 5.2
> Yuan, I will sell it immediately.

Qian regards his position as a guesser and a professional have-less
as a risk. He and other professional have-lesses use the term "blindly
guessing" to describe their investment process, which is insecure and
unstable because there are no patterns, rules, or theories for them to
ensure accuracy. He also used the metaphor of gambling to refer to his
practice of guessing, the accuracy of which depends on uncertain luck.
These professional have-lesses do not usually trust their decisions, which
causes a high level of speculation. Mr. Qian said, "I don't dare to put my
money in the stock market for a long time. If I luckily make some quick
bucks, I sell the stocks." These guessers describe their short-term trading
practices after guessing as speculation and attach meanings like "quick
buy and sell" or "blindly guessing" to the concept.

At this point, it is quite clear that the new risk hierarchy in the ICT
era lies in the gap between "analyzing" and "guessing" and that the
professional have-lesses face uncertainty while the professional have-
mores enjoy a degree of security. In addition, it is assumed that people
in this era should be guided back to the ideal communication process of
financial investment mentioned in Chapter 3 by Mr. Gao: They obtain
the relevant information at hand first, make sense of the information with
expertise, and finally, do their trading based on their own professional
predictions. Those who fail to do so, though they are included in the
game by ICTs, will eventually and reasonably entrust their investments
with experts who can deal with financial investment and offer a sense
of security. A professional-oriented risk culture should be developed in
terms of stock investors. Institutional and professional individuals are
the major communicators in China's stock market, as in other more
mature financial markets. It is also assumed that Western finance companies, which are regarded as more professional and experienced than
Chinese ones, should win the trust in risk communication, like they do
in Hong Kong and Taiwan.

But this surprisingly does not happen. Once included in the game,
the small investors in China do not let go of their mobile phones, PCs,
and iPads. They insist on being part of the communication process in
stock investment, causing excessive speculations in the markets. Many

researchers in finance have pointed out that some investor behavior may come from overconfidence (Caballé & Sákovics, 1996, 2003; Kyle & Wang, 1997; Barber & Odean, 2001; Chen et al., 2007). They overestimate their abilities, blindly believing that they can interpret the stock quotes and predict market tendencies correctly. Such overconfidence eventually causes the investors to suffer from financial risk (Barber et al., 2008). Other studies focus on the greediness of investors (Westerhoff, 2004; Lo, Repin, & Steenbarger, 2005; Partnoy, 2010), noting that they are too eager to earn money from the markets, to the point that they *seek* financial risk instead of avoiding it. When investors' predictions turn out to be wrong, they quickly go from speculation to hotheaded panic selling. All in all, it is easy to jump to the conclusion that not-so-professional individuals play the stock market purely due to their irrationality, similar to gambling addicts (Goodie, 2005; Camchong et al., 2007).

In my opinion, to really understand the reason behind the investors' insistence, we need to look at the communication process of stock investment again. Stock quotes are not the only type of information that the investors communicate and care about, and they are not the only type of information leading to the generation of trading orders. This chapter will focus on two types of information, namely, national affairs and company news. In so doing, this chapter aims to provide insights into the obstacles of the professional-oriented risk culture in China's stock market, as well as the role of digital media in forming this climate.

National Affairs

Big or small, professional or amateur, all investors involved in this book project agreed on two things: the absolute power of the Chinese government on the economy at large, and the willingness of the government to control the national markets. Such belief is consistent with majority of the long-term observers of China (i.e. Unger & Chan, 1995; Qian & Weingast, 1996; Nee, 2000; Lai, 2006). As a result, it is no surprise that Chinese investors perceive news of national affairs to be extremely crucial in stock investment. They identify two different types of national affairs reported in the media: national policies (guojiazhengce) and national economic reports (jingjibaogao). For the investors, national policies include irregular releases of government regulations and laws. It also includes the "attitudes" reflected in discussions taking place about national strategies amongst high-ranked government officers or even statements about future plans from government institutes. As described by the investors, some national policies are pieces of clear and directional information that can guide the investors' future stock trading practices. They can skip the practice of making sense of the stock quotes, jumping straight into trading practices merely based on national policies. For example, Ms. Yu had this to say:

> I am mostly concerned about big national policies. For instance, if President Xi Jingping shows his support for certain industries or companies, the prices of the relevant stocks will increase…If the government increases the duty rate and tries to calm down the market, it is a dangerous sign that we need to 'run away' from the market as fast as possible.

When talking about these national policies, the investors use the terms "nation" and "government"; sometimes they use the terms "party" or "President Xi Jingping" as well. These terms are interchangeable, and all refer to China's authoritarian government, which is seen as having influential, strong, and overwhelming political power over the capital market. The big investors associate all national policies with either encouraging stock investment and supporting certain industries, "bull news" (liduoxiaoxi), or discouraging stock investment and withdrawing support from certain industries, "bear news" (likongxiaoxi). Such news regarding national policies is supposed to be the government's ultimate tool for "guiding" the market at will.

But how do the investors, especially the professional have-mores, feel about this type of information? Gao, a senior analyst, likes to use the term "out of nowhere" to describe the national policies' impact on the market and on their fund.

> They release some bull news out of nowhere. And sometimes they release bear news out of nowhere. Once I saw a notification jump out on a mobile phone screen, which was completely bear news regarding real estate trading. And at that time, we had just completed a brief meeting about the strategy (for the next investment). What a disaster.

Mr. Gao's peer, Mr. Liang, works for another fund and agrees that the "out of nowhere" national policies make him feel that "there is no security at all."

But what does "out of nowhere" mean? According to the investors, it first indicates the sudden and random release of policies (or "attitudes") from various government authorities in relation to different industries. A typical case is the so-called "530 crisis." At the beginning of 2007, investors in China started to celebrate a bull market, and stock prices rose like crazy. Such conditions lasted until May 2007, when a piece of information was distributed among investors that the Ministry of Finance (MoF) would increase the stamp duty to reduce the risk of a hot market. Soon, however, the media reported that an anonymous officer from the MoF said that such information was not true. "We have never heard of this news. It's purely market rumor,"[3] the officer said firmly. Investors were reassured by this declaration and kept investing in the market. But very late at night on May 29, 2007, the MoF suddenly declared an increased stamp duty, which was major bear news for the market at that time. The newspapers were not able to relay the news the next day due to the late-night announcement (some people insisted that the MoF intended to release the news at that late hour). However, the news still broke on the Internet, on TV programs, and on radio channels. Investors fled. The policy actually provoked the financial disaster that it intended to stop, to the point that in June, the government stepped in to release some bull news to stabilize the market.

Ten years later, the 530 disaster still casts a heavy shadow on the trust relationship between the investors and the authorities. The investors jokingly refer to the incident as the "cock crowing at midnight." Huang, the small investor, lost almost half of his savings to that crisis. He was still furious when discussing it with me: "I was so pissed off. They lied to us. You see the Everbright case. They fooled us again and again. I was pissed off that I was fooled again." Liang, a big investor, was busy checking the stock quotations for foreign markets on 29 May. He declared that he was among the first to hear the news because he stayed up all night. "It was like an earthquake. I called my colleagues one by one. It was a lesson, a bitter one. Since then, I always think twice when the officers say something."

Though the "political risk" is high in China's stock markets, it is interesting that such risk is communicated in a rather equal way in the digital media age. No matter what national policies the government releases, the information reaches its receivers through mass communication, either from traditional media outlets or new media; with the Internet, it is impossible for some investors to obtain such news quicker than others and then react to it more quickly. People obtain policy information swiftly from the news reports or the government officials' social network accounts. They then spread it to chat groups, forums, social networks, and news Apps. If we think about how that notification rang out on Mr. Gao's mobile phone, it becomes apparent that national news *approaches* investors, instead of the other way around. Even non-ICT users like Ms. Li, who are possibly information laggards, can catch up with others by exchanging "little favors" with ICT users. Technically speaking, there is little room for any group to take advantage of others regarding the speed of obtaining information about national policies.

The second meaning attached to the term "out of nowhere" refers to the unpredictability of national policies. Even the professional have-mores cannot predict such information using their expertise. Ms. Yu, who labels herself as a "liberalist," said in a very straightforward tone that she thinks some policies are not necessarily "rational decisions" from an economist's perspective. In the context of an authoritarian society, it is difficult for professional investors to use their expertise to predict national policies such as fiscal policies or public investment.

Risk emerges from the resulting sense of powerlessness: what they have learned from textbooks and academic journals does not work in facing the financial world of Chinese society. Mr. Zeng, a junior analyst and stock commentator, used a bitter tone while reflecting on how he feels about the special economic system:

> You thought we had a market economy? I told you, our economy is a strange state-oriented economy. Worse than that, I think someone who does not have knowledge about economics at all plans our economy. The interest groups care only about their own interests.

To be fair, Zeng's accusation is not necessarily true, but it illustrates the common opinion or stereotype of policy makers among investors, that they just "disrupt the market" (from Mr. Liang) instead of controlling risk. Though they question the government's expertise, the professional have-mores are forced to position themselves as followers when obtaining information about national policies and trading stocks following these policies, because of their belief in the government's power to control. For example, Mr. Chen, a big investor, labeled himself a "small potato" (laobaixing) in the eyes of the government:

> Personally, I believe in a free market, but what can I do? I have to follow the government's policies, or I will lose. I am just a small potato...Yes, I have a lot of money, but then what? Faced with the government, my money means nothing...It's like banging your head against a wall.

For the professional have-mores, what makes it worse is that their sensemaking of national policies does not guarantee them a more secure place in financial communication. Simply put, making sense of national policies requires little expertise. For example, Mr. Chen stated, "Even an idiot knows what the government wants (from the news of national affairs)" because "the messages are always very clear." Little cooking skill is required to transform the raw data into directional information for trading, because the information itself is very directional and straightforward.

In other words, the practice of making sense of national policies seems to produce equality, in the sense that those who obtain news about national policies would probably make sense of them in the same way and reach the same judgment about whether a policy is bull or bear news. This condition also indicates that investors with no educational background are professional have-lesses instead of have-nots. For example, Huang, a small investor with absolutely no training in finance and economics, talked fluently about his views regarding the reduction of the required reserve ratio from the People's Bank of China (PBC).

He noted that he compares his opinion with the online discussions when he's not 100% sure. Apart from this situation, it is true that the release of national policies poses a major risk for the professional have-lesses. As Qian, another small investor, told me, "I am nervous about the new government's policy. Different political leaders treat the market differently." But at least such risk is distributed equally between the rich and poor, experts and nonexperts, in the ICT era. There is even a "chance" for the professional have-lesses to catch up with the have-mores, filling in the gap of years of professional training. The equal risk from the political end is somehow a "chance" for the poor to catch up with the rich, too. As Xia, a college student and small investor, puts it, "There is no chance for the bankers to fight against the government. And they would not. Somehow their move is predictable under the release of the (national policy) news."

But are the investors simply weak followers of the government policies as they declare to be? Crisis after crisis, crash after crash, people question the role that government plays in risk communication, first silently in the mass media era but later more vocally during the digital age. For example, the 530 crisis mentioned above triggered tremendous opposition (and it was communicated online). Netizens still mention it from time to time whenever an issue about government trust arises. Another typical case emerged during the 2016 Circuit Breaker Crisis. In 2015, due to the market crashes in the same year, the Shanghai Stock Exchange (SSE), Shenzhen Stock Exchange (SZSE), and China Financial Futures Exchange issued a new policy named the "circuit breaker mechanism" with the approval of China Securities Regulatory Commission (CSRC). The policy itself was very straightforward. The circuit breaker was based upon a stock market index called CSI 300, a replication of the performance of 3,000 select stocks from the SSE and SZSE. A 15-minute market suspension would be launched if there was a 5% rise or fall in the CSI 300 index. And a 7% rise or fall in the same index would result in a suspension of the stock markets for the whole trading day. It was declared that this policy was for "stabilizing the market" and "controlling systematic risk." In addition, it was designed following similar rules as those appearing in the more professional financial markets of the West.

Many profession have-mores did not buy these statements; however, Ms. Yu said,

> I think there is a huge misunderstanding. Do they realize there are many differences between abroad and China's financial markets? ... Besides, they use the one-shot case in the US market in the 1980s to legitimize a similar policy being applied to China in 2016? And this is called 'learning from the professional systems'? It makes no sense to me.

Mr. Chen, who was even more critical, said angrily, "I doubt they know what a 'systematic risk' is and is not. I doubt they even know who Markowitz is." Some experts started to publish blogs, and microbloggers voiced their concerns, while the professional have-lesses were torn between different opinions. For example, Mr. Huang, a small investor, said that he was "totally at a loss" because he "did not know what the hell a circuit breaker mechanism was."

Despite the doubts from the professional end, the government still issued the rule "after a public hearing," and the policy was applied at the beginning of 2016. Against the government's good intentions, the circuit breaker mechanism resulted in market panic in the first few days of its launching, causing market suspensions twice within four days. Both professional have-mores and have-nots, the wealthy and the poor, joined in an online protest against the policy. Tremendous numbers of posts and blogs burst out in cyberspace. The voice of the defenders was too weak to hear over the furious roars. Facing the public outcry, the CSRC had to suspend its policy after only four days of application. Xiao Gang, the head of the CSRC, was removed from his position shortly after the incident. Even in liberal societies, it is rare to see political leaders in finance actually pay for their policy faults—and with not a single person walking onto the streets to protest. The interviewed investors thought that the policy would not have been so easy to terminate without the digital challenges coming out against the policy. Mr. Liang, who posted several hot microblogs criticizing the circuit breaker mechanism himself, said to me, "Without the Internet, the issues could be calmed down easily. At least Xiao Gang would not have been removed so fast, I think."

As discussed in Chapter 1, back in the 1990s, a news article was published stating that the mouthpiece of the government could easily guide the direction of the market. But in 2015, similar calls from the government through mass media received few answers from investors. During the 530 crisis, though people believed in the power of the government, they did not believe in its expertise. In the digital media era, such distrust has been expanded in a more collective way. Put another way, news releases regarding policies still impact the market, but they are not accepted silently without struggles and denials.

National Economic Reports

If national policies reflect the government's will, national economic reports indicate—or should indicate—the factual conditions of the national market. Ms. Yu explained the importance of national economic reports from her professional perspective as follows:

> By its very nature, the stock market cannot be isolated from the national economy. In theory, if the nation's economy is very healthy,

some of the listed companies have a better chance for good performance. It suggests that the more faith people have in the national economy, the more faith they have in the future of some listed companies...They (economic reports) are like weather forecasts for the market.

In stark contrast to the irregularly released national policies, national economic reports appear regularly, providing information on national economic matters from government departments or other important financial institutions. These reports represent another type of national affairs news that investors care about and communicate during the investing process. These reports are, in general, about past or future conditions in the Chinese economy, and they get released monthly, seasonally, or yearly by government institutions such as the National Bureau of Statistics of China, the PBC, the MoF of China, and the Ministry of Commerce of China. Mr. Qian, who does not use ICTs, described how he obtains economic reports through mass media:

I get to know the GDP index by watching TV. There are monthly news reports about the GDP. I always forget what the abbreviations mean, you know, but the reporters explain them briefly when reporting the news. So I can at least have a general idea if the national economy is good or bad. Sometimes I forget the details of the TV news, or I forget to watch TV news. So I read the newspapers to learn what is going on in our country. The newspapers mention these reports in more detail, but usually they only quote part of the reports.

Qian evaluates the practice of watching TV as a satisfactory method of obtaining and making sense of the national economic reports, because it satisfies the criteria of "speediness" and "accuracy" in obtaining news. Theoretically, people using the Internet should be one step faster than the non-ICT users in obtaining the national economic reports; however, because releases occur following a routine schedule, the non-ICT users can catch up easily by setting up a viewing schedule to obtain such information. For Mr. Qian and the small investors who are non-ICT users, their worries regarding "the risk of being left behind" (Ms. Li) are eased by the conceptualization of equality.

However, the investors also evaluated the practice of watching TV as ineffective because they cannot sustain their freedom in controlling the practice. They cannot repeatedly watch the national economic reports news anytime they like. In addition, the criterion of "completeness" or "exhaustion" is left unsatisfied by the practice of watching TV. The national economic reports usually are described as lengthy and complicated, and according to the investors, TV news broadcasts, which are limited in length, usually only quote a segment of the reports. The newspapers describe the national economic reports with more detail, but the content is still incomplete. For non-ICT users, this omitted information is a huge risk, because they could be missing some important messages.

ICT users, on the other hand, evaluate their practice of surfing the Internet as satisfactory because the practice satisfies the criterion of "completeness" in obtaining news about national economic reports. By positioning themselves as ICT users, the investors actively evaluate and use online information sources to ensure that they do not miss any important information, thus making certain that they obtain more information about the national economy than others do. Further, by using ICT, the ICT users exercise freedom in controlling the practice, which is associated with security for them. For example, Zeng told me how he obtains information from websites when we were sitting in his office:

> You see that? I check the official websites of the financial institutions of government departments for the full reports. Can you see the column entitled 'news releases'? Let me click that. There it is. I can read and reread it anytime I want. Sometimes the news websites will release the full reports as well. The news reports (on TV) are too general. I always check the full reports and analyze them.

When I asked Zeng what he meant by the term "too general" when referring to TV news reporting of national economic reports, he stated that the TV news programs try to provide the most crucial information from the reports; in doing so, they miss other information and focus too much on the whole national economy. Other professional have-mores agreed that they would like to obtain detailed data about the specific industries, distinguishing between bull news and bear news for a particular group of companies. The reason for this specificity can be seen in the fact that the stock performance of certain listed companies could be more sensitive to partial aspects of the economic reports, instead of the national economy on a grand scale. Such "determination" and "specification" processes require a professional background; in other words, it is a communication practice of professional analysis instead of a blind guess. This situation grants the professional have-mores—most of whom are also ICT users obtaining complete economic reports—a privileged position in communicating the state's economic conditions and its relationship to stock market performance. Those who are non-ICT users or professional have-lesses admit that they are underdogs. They find their evaluation unsatisfactory for either obtaining or making sense of national economic reports. A sense of risk emerges from such difficulties, and thus, they feel left behind, often encouraging a "practice-shifting moment." They may begin to turn to other people for help, seeking "cooked" information like stock opinion and stock comments (which will be analyzed in Chapter 6).

As a result, the communication of national economic reports should facilitate a professional-oriented risk culture in the ICT era due to its complicated and lengthy nature. But is that truly the case? The professional have-mores and ICT users, who should feel secure in communicating such information, are shockingly insecure about the national economy. Let's look back to the beginning of this section, when Ms. Yu said, "In theory, if the nation's economy is very healthy, some of the listed companies have a better chance for good performance." The term "in theory" may shed light on the experts' concerns. I asked her what she meant by "in theory."

> It means that the conditions just happen in ideal circumstances. You know, some people do not trust the economic reports. I am not sure, but you know, the local government officials would like the data to be polished so that they can remain in their positions or get promotions. It is possible that they fake the data. Corruption and cheating happens in our society, so it is possible…Indeed, we invest in them just because the stock price has a better chance of increasing due to the (broad casting of) bull news. We do not really have faith in the economy or in these companies.

For the investors, when basic economic information is biased, their ability to accurately predict future economic conditions is lower. Professional have-mores face risk due to their distrust in the government's expertise. This risk is double when they also question the honesty of the authorities communicating these national economic reports. They are forced to consider the possibility of a corrupt political system while making sense of information that they do not trust. Thus, the investors told me that they would buy and sell stocks quickly after making sense of the national economic reports, acting on the assumption that other investors would speculate in the market following the national reports; they take such actions instead of believing that the reports reflect actual future tendencies in the national economy and particular listed companies. "If data is really reliable, we would like to make long-term investments. Who would not want to? It's more stable," Mr. Chen the big investor told me, "But I am not sure about these figures. We have to speculate, earn money, and withdraw quickly."

Excessive speculation is one thing, but another more serious problem is the separation between the economic conditions from the stock quote tendencies. The investors suffered almost five years of a bear market in China from the end of 2000 to 2005, with the index of A-share dropping from 2073 to 1161. But during the same period, the Chinese economy as a whole soared, maintaining 8–10% growth per year. It is hard to say which comes first, the chicken or the egg. Is the problem the distrust toward the economic reports or the separation of economic conditions

from actual stock market performance? One thing is for sure: the professional have-mores are no more able to construct security by making
sense of the economic reports. What makes things worse is that many
of them are not able to—or reluctant to—speak publicly about their
distrust. As Liang told me,

> I represent my fund and my company. I shall be cautious when
> talking. It's something you keep to yourself or discuss in the meet-
> ing room. It is another thing to write about it on a blog or discuss it
> on a TV show.

But Liang is not reluctant to criticize financial policies, and actually, he
was one of the fiercest online opponents of the circuit breaker policy from
CSRC back in 2016. "To question a policy is easy, but to point fingers at
corruption is not. We need hard evidence, you know," Liang said.

Meanwhile, ICT platforms seem to provide these small investors a
chance to question the economic conditions. Throughout the interviews,
the majority of investors declared that they actually believe in the central
government, but have grave concerns about some local governments.
Interestingly, running contrary to assumptions that China's cyberspace
is completely censored, there is room for people to voice their critiques
in relation to national affairs, especially regarding economic topics.
Xia, a college student, posted in several forums and Weibo platforms
questioning one county-level government's GDP report:

> I grew up there. I know those officials. I know what is going on in
> my hometown. The economy sucks. Corruption is everywhere. The
> local bureau is doing nothing. I want the central government and the
> public to know what's going on.

Mr. Huang, a small investor, was also not shy in expressing his view
of the economy in WeChat groups and forums: "We are complaining
for the good of the country," Huang said, "and it is interesting to see
how other people respond to my critiques." By positioning themselves
as the questioners, the small investors who are ICT users seem to have
more freedom than the big ones in communicating about the national
economy.

The political regime's tolerance of publicly communicated distrust
toward the GDP probably rests in the fact that the central government
holds the same doubts as Xia and Huang. Such double was not from
vacuum. The extent to which China's economic data is correct remains a
topic of long-term discussion—with a lot of question marks. The underlying reason for such suspicion comes from the political system of China.
The system basically applies an authoritarian mechanism, as a result of
the fact that "the politicians are held accountable to their supervisors

rather than to the public" (Cai, 2004, p. 22). "Supervisors" here refers to government officials with a higher rank in the local or central government. They evaluate the performance of those below them and have the authority to promote or demote them (Ran, 2013). Consequently, it has become crucial to satisfy the requirements coming from above, particularly for politicians working within the system. They have to satisfy their superiors in order to survive and advance in their careers.

Since the economic reforms and open door policy were introduced at the end of the 1970s, the Communist Party's biggest political goal and promise has been "building up a moderately prosperous society" (Hu, 2007, 2012). Economic growth has become the dominant criterion in the eyes of China's political leaders when judging their subordinates (Gao, 2015). As a result of this cadre evaluation system and other political pressures, local officials started to artificially inflate GDP data (see Wu, 1997; Chow & Li, 2002; Cai, 2004; Carsten, 2004; Holz, 2014), trying to deceive the central government. The central government has become aware of this situation because of the discrepancies between the GDP calculated by the National Bureau of Statistics and the cumulative data reported from the local governments. The inconsistencies reached ridiculously high levels in 2012 and 2013. The media reported that the discrepancy was 5.76 trillion and 6.19 trillion RMB, respectively, exceeding 10% of the entire GDP volume.[4] Journalists came to the conclusion that this gap also might result from technical differences between the National Bureau of Statistics and local governments in calculating data. In recent years, due to pressure from the central regime, several local governments have taken a more open attitude, starting to admit that the economic growth data had been overinflated. The province-level governments like Liaoning and the city-level and smaller levels like Baotou and Tianjin Binhai had taken on a "water squeeze" strategy (which means to "squeeze out" the false data from GDP) to revise their former statistical data.[5] Due to these scandals, it will take time to win back public trust for national economic reports.

International News

By now, the readers may already see the difficulties that the Chinese professional have-mores face when communicating national affairs. Similar problems arise for international finance companies as well, though they are perceived as more experienced and professional. Their estimation of a listed company or a market as a whole could stimulate a dramatic response from the Hong Kong and Taiwan stock markets. Whenever they raise a red flag, investors in these areas are prepared to run away from the emerging risk. However, these companies' reports usually are met with total indifference in mainland China. Mr. Gao, a senior analyst, puts it simply, "They (the international finance companies) do not know the games we play." This statement is generally agreed upon by almost all the investors with whom I talked. The professional have-nots would choose a local stock commentator from a fund or even another professional have-not who's delivering unreliable "insider information" over the professional analysis of a world-famous finance company. This choice does not reflect irrationality; rather, they do not believe that the international finance companies can understand national affairs in China better than the local people. The assumed advantage in expertise does not work here.

But how about another advantage that the international finance companies have: a supposed global version of financial knowledge? Industries and academia alike discuss the compression of the world's space all the time, especially regarding global risk. This observation is true in China because its economy cannot be separated from the world market. World economic catastrophes, like the subprime mortgage crisis and the European debt crisis, all have had major impacts on China's economic entities. Because events in the global financial world affect China's economy in general and stock markets in particular, international finance companies definitely could grab a privileged position in risk communication, declaring that they are more familiar with global economics and finance.

Surprisingly, such presumptions do not happen in China. To understand why, we need to look at the communication of one type of investor information, international news. If the communication of national affairs is a must-have for Chinese investors, international news is only considered such by a fraction of the investors. Ms. Lin, a small investor, explained to me why she does not regard international news as crucial for stock investment:

> People always say globalization, globalization, globalization. Yes, our economy is globalized. But our market is not globalized. It is closed. Foreign investment is highly restricted... I think that national news is more important. The global issues are too distant. The stock prices are not very sensitive to them...Even though they influence some listed companies, I can't tell which ones by myself. I read the stock commentary about the international news as reference.

From this typical description, we can see that investors do not deny the impact of global events on the local economy—what they deny is the directional influence of global capital on local stock markets. And, it's the latter that reduces the discourse power of foreign finance companies in risk communication in China. What also lies behind this statement is the separation of economic conditions and stock performance that we have discussed in this chapter. Due to this separation, investors in China have become the ultimate believers in "behavioral finance." They focus not on theory but on what other investors, especially "bankers," will do.

Here, "bankers" refer to the controllers of local finance companies and funds in China. So far, the foreign companies are never the predominant bankers in China's stock markets—nor are they (believed to be) familiar with the behaviors of local bankers. Of course, many global finance companies today seek to join the Qualified Foreign Institutional Investor (QFII) Scheme.[6] The 2002 launch of the State Administration of Foreign Exchange's (SAFE) "Provisional Measures on Administration of Domestic Securities Investments of Qualified Foreign Institutional Investors (QFII)" has allowed foreign institutional investors to invest in China's stock market in a limited manner. More than a decade later, the Chinese government has largely increased its quotas and the amount of money allowable through the QFII scheme. The latest report from SAFE[7] indicates that up to March 2018, China allowed 287 foreign financial institutions to invest in the local financial markets, with a total quota of 994.59 billion USD. Leading figures like UBS, Morgan Stanley, Citigroup, Goldman Sachs, and Deutsche Bank have all been included on the list. However, the average capital permitted does not allow them to become effective manipulators. In addition, the Chinese government places a number of restrictions on these companies. For example, in its regulations and guidelines for QFII investors putting money into China's stock index futures,[8] the CSRC makes it very clear that "(we) don't encourage arbitraging or speculation among the QFII investors...The QFII investors are only allowed to do hedging." This situation, accompanied by their inability (in Chinese investors' opinion) to make sense of China's national affairs, excludes them from a privileged place in financial risk communication. As Chen, a big investor, puts it, stock investment and its communication process in China is a "game only for insiders."

Interestingly, though the professional have-nots do not consider it crucial to watch international news or listen to the analysis of global finance companies, as Lin said, they do value the local professional have-mores' comments regarding such information. "It's proof that the stock commentators are professional and convincing, that they at least can read those complicated reports," says Mr. Huang a small investor. Huang's statement was confirmed by the professional have-mores, especially those more socially vocal ones. These investors seek to obtain and make sense of international news through the practice of sharing stock opinions or stock comments; it is not required by the practice of predicting stock quotes in the short term. Mr. Gao, a senior analyst and stock commentator, told me the following:

> Every professional analyst needs to pay attention to the international news. I do not believe that it has a direct influence on our market, but it affects some of our industries long-term, and eventually it is reflected in the financial statements of the listed companies...Also, as a stock commentator, I frequently mention my analyses on the international news. I check first-hand business news every day on

English news websites. It shows my professionalism. My biggest fear is that my clients will not trust me. I need to show them my professionalism to make them trust me.

Not only Gao, but also Zeng, Liang, and Yu mentioned the term "first-hand" (diyishou) to describe the international news they obtain. For these professional have-mores, the term has two meanings. First, the international news they obtain is probably the latest news, not reposted information. Using ICTs, the professional have-mores are able to obtain the latest news. They mention that obtaining the latest international news means that they can make sense of it quicker than others, and by doing so, they can position themselves as professional analysts who share stock comments or opinions that most other people do not know. Second, it means that they must have the ability to read foreign languages (like English) to obtain the news since the original sources are not in Chinese. For the investors, the English language requirement is also associated with their position as professional analysts. For example, Ms. Li, a small investor, stated that she respects experts who can use English because English learning in China is associated with a high level of education (McKay, 2002).

The professional have-mores, especially those who work as stock analysts or stock commentators, associate people's distrust toward them with risk. They construct security by obtaining the latest international news using their foreign language ability, making sense of it by identifying the influence of international issues on the national market, using their professional background in finance, and sharing their professional opinions about international news. In essence, they reinforce and reproduce their position as professional have-mores, which is linked to the people's trust in them. Like small investors, they believe that international news has little direct effect on China's financial market. As a result, obtaining and making sense of international news does not directly link with the professional have-mores' practice of trading stocks. It's more like a polishing practice that adds to their professional profile.

So far, we have seen an interesting contradiction in the risk culture of Chinese stock markets. People very much realize that professionalism is dismantled in the face of major political risks regarding national affairs. Sometimes, however, they still want the privileged groups in risk communication to have at least some level of expertise. This desire is challenged further when they communicate company information and stock commentary, as will be analyzed in Chapters 5 and 6, respectively.

Notes

1 An order book is the list recording intended buying and selling, indicating the trading orders entering the market system (Biais, Hillion, & Spatt, 1995; Gu, Chen, & Zhou, 2007).

2 A limit order refers to a trading order set to be executed at a certain price. It includes sell limit orders and buy limit orders (see Ahn, Bae, & Chan, 2001; Aitken, Berkman, & Mak, 2001; Chung, Van Ness, & Van Ness, 1999 for reference).

3 See http://business.sohu.com/20070523/n250174639.shtml

4 See www.sohu.com/a/217309827_313480. According to China's National Bureau of Statistics, in 2012, the GDP of China was 51.93 trillion RMB, while the total GDP of the local governments was 57.69 trillion RMB. The numbers were 56.88 and 63.07 trillion RMB, respectively, in 2013. According to the data retrieved from the official website of the National Bureau of Statistics in China (www.stats.gov.cn/tjsj/), the finalized GDP was 54.04 trillion RMB in 2012 and 59.52 trillion RMB in 2013, somehow higher than the original versions. However, the huge discrepancy between the national and local data remains.

5 See www.reuters.com/article/us-china-economy-data/another-chinese-city-admits-fake-economic-data-idUSKBN1F60I1

6 See www.csrc.gov.cn/pub/csrc_en/newsfacts/release/200708/t20070810_69192.html

7 See www.safe.gov.cn/wps/wcm/connect/5de310804dc4fdaea779a7a46e1b18c9/合格境外机构投资者（QFII）投资额度审批情况表（截至2018年03月29日）.pdf

8 See www.csrc.gov.cn/zjhpublic/.../P020110125618318906278.doc

References

Barber, B. M., & Odean, T. (2001). Boys will be boys: Gender, overconfidence, and common stock investment. *The Quarterly Journal of Economics*, *116*(1), 261–292.

Barber, B. M., Lee, Y. T., Liu, Y. J., & Odean, T. (2008). Just how much do individual investors lose by trading? *The Review of Financial Studies*, *22*(2), 609–632.

Caballé, J., & Sákovics, J. (1996). *Overconfident speculation with imperfect competition* (UFAE and IAE Working Papers No. 336.96). Unitat de Fonaments de l'Anàlisi Econòmica (UAB) and Institut d'Anàlisi Econòmica (CSIC).

Caballé, J., & Sákovics, J. (2003). Speculating against an overconfident market. *Journal of Financial Markets*, *6*(2), 199–225.

Cai, Y. (2004). Irresponsible state: Local cadres and image-building in China. *Journal of Communist Studies and Transition Politics*, *20*(4), 20–41.

Camchong, J., Goodie, A. S., McDowell, J. E., Gilmore, C. S., & Clementz, B. A. (2007). A cognitive neuroscience approach to studying the role of overconfidence in problem gambling. *Journal of Gambling Studies*, *23*(2), 185–199.

Carsten, A. H. (2004). Deconstructing China's GDP statistics. *China Economic Review*, *15*(2), 164–202.

Chen, G., Kim, K. A., Nofsinger, J. R., & Rui, O. M. (2007). Trading performance, disposition effect, overconfidence, representativeness bias, and experience of emerging market investors. *Journal of Behavioral Decision Making*, *20*(4), 425–451.

Chow, G. C., & Li, K. W. (2002). China's economic growth: 1952–2010. *Economic Development and Cultural Change*, *51*(1), 247–256.

Gao, J. (2015). Pernicious manipulation of performance measures in China's cadre evaluation system. *The China Quarterly*, *223*, 618–637.

Goodie, A. S. (2005). The role of perceived control and overconfidence in pathological gambling. *Journal of Gambling Studies, 21*(4), 481–502.

Holz, C. A. (2014). The quality of China's GDP statistics. *China Economic Review, 30*, 309–338.

Hu, J. (2007). Hold high the great banner of socialism with Chinese characteristics and strive for new victories in building a moderately prosperous society in all respects. *China Daily*, 2007–2010. Retrieved from www.lancaster.ac.uk/fass/projects/ndcc/download/17thcongress.pdf

Hu, J. (2012, November). Firmly march on the path of socialism with Chinese characteristics and strive to complete the building of a moderately prosperous society in all respects. In *A collection of documents of the 18th CPC National Congress.*

Kyle, A. S., & Wang, F. A. (1997). Speculation duopoly with agreement to disagree: Can overconfidence survive the market test? *The Journal of Finance, 52*(5), 2073–2090.

Lai, H. (2006). *Reform and the non-state economy in China: The political economy of liberalization strategies.* New York: Palgrave Macmillan.

Lo, A. W., Repin, D. V., & Steenbarger, B. N. (2005). Fear and greed in financial markets: A clinical study of day-traders. *American Economic Review, 95*(2), 352–359.

McKay, S. L. (2002). *Teaching English as an international language: Rethinking goals and perspectives.* New York: Oxford University Press.

Nee, V. (2000). The role of the state in making a market economy. *Journal of Institutional and Theoretical Economics (JITE)/Zeitschrift für die gesamte Staatswissenschaft, 156*, 64–88.

Partnoy, F. (2010). *Infectious greed: How deceit and risk corrupted the financial markets.* London: Profile Books.

Qian, Y., & Weingast, B. R. (1996). China's transition to markets: Market-preserving federalism, Chinese style. *The Journal of Policy Reform, 1*(2), 149–185.

Ran, R. (2013). Perverse incentive structure and policy implementation gap in China's local environmental politics. *Journal of Environmental Policy & Planning, 15*(1), 17–39.

Unger, J., & Chan, A. (1995). China, corporatism, and the East Asian model. *The Australian Journal of Chinese Affairs, 33*, 29–53.

Westerhoff, F. H. (2004). Greed, fear and stock market dynamics. *Physica A: Statistical Mechanics and Its Applications, 343*, 635–642.

Wu, H. X. (1997). *Measuring China's GDP* (No. 8). Canberra: East Asia Analytical Unit, Department of Foreign Affairs and Trade.

5 Communicating Company Information

When talking about the risk in communicating national affairs, Mr. Liang, a big investor, casually said, "If it's about a company's statues, maybe I can find a *solution* (to verify that). But who the hell knows the real conditions of our nation?"

This statement is quite interesting if we take a deeper look. What Liang has referred to as "a company's statues" is coded as *company information* in my research. Alongside national affairs, this term refers to the most important sought-after information. When describing national affairs news—whether referring to national policies or to national economic reports—investors typically use general terms like "China," "the national economy," "the market," and "the industry" to describe the massive influence of this type of information on stock investments. Nevertheless, when describing company news—business news related to market-listed companies—investors tend to mention the specific names of the companies being reported on. When making sense of company news, there is no need to specify or narrow down the information in order to identify the specific companies in question; indeed, the target companies are always mentioned clearly in the message. In the ideal form of risk communication in finance, company news should serve as a guide for the market, guaranteeing that the money flows to the most promising companies.

But such financial utopia faces an enemy. Liang's statement may provide a clue. For investors, one important difference between national affairs communication and company news is whether or not there is a "solution"; in Liang's words, such an approach would involve seeking more secure information. It is crystal clear that the political risk to investors, the uncertainties in national affairs communication, is distributed in a somewhat equal way. Investors in China—especially the liberal ones—do complain about the governance structure; however, they simultaneously maintain faith that the government is too powerful to be bought easily. For example, Ms. Yu described the higher risk of insider information trading for companies compared to national affairs:

> It (national policy leaks) does happen world-wide, but the risk is high (for both sides) in China's financial world. You know, the big

bankers keep an eye on each other. The CSRC keeps an eye on the big bankers. If a fund manager is playing tricks with a government official, say, reacting faster than us before a policy is released, and it happens several times, they are playing with fire and crossing the line ... But the exchange of insider information (of company news) is harder to detect. And I have to admit that it's much easier for the big capitalists to reach the companies than the government authorities using *guanxi* (personal relations/social capital).

What Yu describes in this last part of her statement expresses the "solution" for many big investors: They position themselves as market bribers and manipulators, communicating insider information regarding company news. It's no wonder such practices corrode the professionally oriented risk culture of the financial world. But why do the big investors play this game? As discussed in the previous chapter, the majority of big investors are professional have-mores. It is reasonable to assume that they can take advantage of their expertise in communicating company news, earning a privileged position in evaluating the risk and chances of success for a listed company. Could it be that Chinese big investors are too greedy to use their expertise to invest in a decent company for the long term? Meanwhile, what is the small investor's reaction to such conditions in the digital age? To answer these questions, we first have to define company news further. Then, we must delineate how different information is communicated through media.

Common Company News and Market Manipulations

Investors' typology of company news is very similar to how they divide national affairs. In general, they conceptualize two types of company news of interest. First, they seek every day, common news about listed companies (which does not include financial statements). The release time of such news tends to be irregular just like the random release of national policies. Examples of such news include mergers, changes in executive staff, bidding results, or scandals that threaten the whole company. The second type of company news includes regular financial statements for listed companies, which are usually audited by accounting firms. This type of information mirrors the seasonal or annual releases of national economic reports.

Generally speaking, due to the specificity of company news, which targets particular securities, stock quotes can be more responsive to national affairs. This truism makes information and communication technologies (ICTs) particularly important because people require the information to be delivered quickly, almost instantly. On the contrary, non-ICT users face a major risk of being left behind in the communication of company news. Mr. Qian, a small investor who does not use ICT, described how he obtains the common news regarding listed companies while sitting in the big stock exchange hall:

> See? There are so many listed companies. I can't focus on all of them. I have to focus on the news (of the companies) I am interested in to see if any news about them turns up in newspapers or TV programs. But I am still worried that I will be the last person to know some important news. You know, breaking news can be released at any time. So, I ask my friends in the stock exchange hall who use computers for help to see if there is any company news.

From Qian's description, we can see that he evaluates the practice of obtaining company news using the criteria of exhaustiveness and speediness; he understands that risk arises when he is uncertain about certain criteria being fulfilled. Qian positions himself as a "selector" by obtaining news about particular companies in response to the risk related to exhaustiveness. Faced with a lack of speed due to the lack of ICT use, he shifts to the practice of making inquiries of ICT users instead of reading newspapers or watching TV. Positioning himself as an inquirer and a friend to ICT users, Qian obtains company news more actively. Such inquiry practices are very much like the exchanging of stock quotes mentioned in Chapter 3. These practices involve small talk about stock, and this communication requires, produces, and/or reinforces interpersonal relationships among the small investors. During the shifting moments of practice, the non-ICT users construct the idea of security as relying on their solid personal relationships with ICT users. Through this practice, they increase their equality and subsequent sense of security.

Mr. Qin, a small investor, usually acts as a sharer of common company news to non-ICT users like Qian. In one interview, Qin mentioned,

> We (small investors in the same stock exchange hall) know each other's investing conditions ... So, when I see some breaking news from news websites or my stock software about the listed companies that my friends have invested some money in, I tell them.

By positioning himself as a deliverer of news, Qin evaluates the sharing practice as satisfactory because sharing news means that he is helpful to and friendly toward other investors. Just like sharing information about stock prices, sharing the latest company news allows the investors to build interpersonal relations with the mutual understanding of favor exchange. These relationships are more cooperative than competitive, producing security for the small investors. Such security in the social network constantly attracts the small investors to the stock exchange hall, though some of them use ICT at home to complete the communication process.

These small investors who exchange information about the common company news also attach meaning to equality in this cooperative relationship. For instance, both Qian, who asks ICT users to help him, and Qin, who is an ICT user sharing company news with non-ICT users, describe the sharing practice as "not a big issue" or merely "a little favor." This description parallels the practice of inquiring and sharing stock prices: The easy accessibility of digital media reduces the rarity of such information. To exchange up-to-date yet publicly communicated company news is not a big deal like it was before the digital age. But how about making sense of it? Is sensemaking regarded as raw information like stock quotes or national economic reports, waiting to be explained and transformed, or as directional information like national policies?

The investors tell me that making sense of common company news means ascertaining whether or not the news is good. Good news about the company encourages investors to invest their money, but bad news may cause investors to withdraw their investments from the company. For some company news, the process of determining whether it is bull news or bear news is so easy that "even idiots can see it." But the professional have-mores, like Mr. Gao, insist that it is only experts that can judge whether or not a company has bull news in the long term. He pointed to his computer while talking to me:

> Look, this is news about a merger negotiation, right? Non-professional investors tend to think it's bull news. But it's too quick to say that. An expert would judge it from different angles. I think there is risk in that (merger). If you get to know the condition of the company, you know that they can't handle the new situation. It's bizarre that they make such decisions. However, considering the small investors' reaction, it's bull news in the short term, for sure.

At this point, we can paint a picture of company news communication. Thanks to ICTs, the practice of obtaining company news has equalized between the rich and poor, the experts and amateurs. With this equal footing, the nonprofessional investors (most of whom are small investors) might even obtain an equal position with the professional ones for the short term when it comes to making sense of company news. Even though their opinions evaluating a company's risk may not be considered professional, the experts still have to take into their ideas into consideration. This truth is apparent because they insist on staying in the market. As readers have already seen in Chapter 3, this insistence is again thanks to ICTs, which facilitate the communication of stock quotes and trading orders among the majority of investors. However, in the long term, the professional have-mores will gradually seize the upper hand in risk communication because they are better equipped to evaluate the risk of a listed company basing on the news.

Ultimately, the professional-oriented risk culture should eventually get the win, but readers already know that it will never happen in China. To understand why, we shall reconsider the term used by small investors Qian and Qin when describing the exchange of company news: "a little favor." This term illustrates the belittling of publicly communicated company news—and it is not just because of easy access to information in the digital age. The reason for this devaluation of company news is twofold: the communication of insider information and market manipulation by big bankers. More specifically, investors communicate company news with the belief that (1) some people might obtain the information before the official release and react faster than the general public, and (2) the news itself could be unreliable because it might be bait from manipulators. The former erodes the security granted by quickly obtaining public company news, and the latter harms the confidence and accuracy in predicting a company's future performance. Qin, a small investor and stock software user, says that even though he can quickly obtain a large amount of recent company news, the practice itself is useless because the news is not reliable. He states very straightforwardly that he does not trust company news at all:

> I was fooled by (company) news several times. They released some bull or bear news just because the bankers wanted to bait us small investors. The media were corrupt. They took bribes from the companies and then released the news containing fake content. . . I trust nothing in (company) news. You know what, if it is bull news, you should be careful. Don't be hot-headed or your money will be stolen by the bankers.

When Qin says "bankers," he uses the metaphor to construct a meaning for the big investors as rich, powerful, and manipulative cheaters. He also uses the metaphor of robbery to construct the big investors' cheating behavior as illegal and unethical. The small investors position themselves as victims who are fooled into the practice of making sense of the common company news, and they position the listed companies, the big investors, and the media as cheats. Owing to the unequal position of the big and small investors, "zero-sum relations" are produced in the sense that the small investors' losses become the big investors' gains. The small investors also make comparisons between national policy news and company news, noting that news about national policies is more reliable. "At least it is difficult for them (the bankers) to buy the central government," says Mr. Qin.

> I can endure the risk of national policies because at least all of the investors are facing some risk. It bothers me that the big investors use their money to manipulate the market, and us small investors are faced with danger.

But what about those big bankers, the investors who have the capability to manipulate small investors' fear, excitement, and uncertainty? It is understandable that big investors are very cautious when talking about this issue. The majority of big investors, especially those who work for financial institutions, deny that they are involved in communicating insider information or manipulating the market. But interestingly, they all admit that they "have heard of" or "know someone" who has participated in these practices. Chen, a big investor, wanted to "share a story, no guarantee if it truly happened or not." The story referred to a banker called X who shared bear news to scare small investors and then buy the stock for a lower price, which is "very common" (Chen) in China's stock market.

> I have heard that X is a good friend of the big boss of S company. They set the whole thing up in advance ... X was manipulating the prices using the money, and he asked his friends in the media (a journalist or a stock commentator) to release bad news. You know, it's easy just to say, 'This company is facing challenges in a foreign market' or some bullshit like that. When the price crashed, X bought in. After that, the company released some bull news to stimulate investment from the market, and then they earned a lot of money from that ... The boss does not care about the company. They all want to earn some quick bucks from the capital market and withdraw from it.

By communicating insider information, producing misleading information, and controlling the stock prices with money, X produced security due to his certainty about the information regarding trends in future stock prices. He also created security by positioning himself as a manipulator and taking advantage of the uncertainty of small investors. However, according to Chen, X simultaneously associates his practices with risk, "All in all, it's not a stable and safe way to make money." Unlike other investors being misled by the company news, X is aware that he has invested in a company with doubtful value. Chen says that X uses the term "rubbish" to describe the company. Thus, his valuation of the company contradicts his trading practice, which leads to his uncertainty. He has to deal with the insecurity of earning a "few quick bucks and withdrawing" from the market. X also is worried that the government could take action against his market manipulation. "Who knows? Maybe X will have bad luck," Chen said.

Even big investors who deny using common stock news to manipulate the market agree on the ubiquity of such practices. Thus, they distrust common stock news as well, thereby producing uncertainty—and a sense of vulnerability because they cannot use expertise to predict future trends more accurately than others. But unlike small investors, the big investors have "solutions." A practice-shifting moment happens in this regards: Big investors quit depending on their profession to judge the risk of a listed company, almost forcing them to use their capital to build up a guanxi network with other businesspeople and bankers. This network is essential in confirming and verifying whether or not a piece of company news is reliable. Because the private information gained by guanxi is considered more accurate than public company news, the exchange of insider information becomes a "big favor." Mr. Liang, a big investor, does not like the "culture" of exchanging insider information at all, but there seems to be little he can do in this guanxi-oriented risk culture:

> It's annoying. It's like your destiny is not in your own hands. I don't like that. But it's a game and you have to follow the rules … If you believe everything that the company publishes, your competitors in other funds will laugh their heads off.

Financial Statements

Another type of company news concerning investors is the company's financial statements. The investors describe financial statements as documents that outline the economic conditions of the target company, documents that are released regularly. Mr. Zeng, a junior stock analyst and commentator, had this to say:

> The government asks all the listed companies to publicize their financial statements seasonally and annually. We all know when they will be released … After the release of the statement, TV news programs, news websites, and social networks report on them immediately … I do not worry about missing this type of information.

Similar to obtaining the common company news, the investors obtain financial statement news from both the mass media and ICTs, practices that satisfy the criterion of speediness while producing a sense of security for both ICT users and non-ICT users. Investors also gain security from the regularity of the release of financial statements for listed companies. However, even though the investors associate the regular release of financial statements for listed companies with the idea of equality between ICT and non-ICT users, the non-ICT users point out that the practice of watching TV news does not satisfy the criterion of completeness in obtaining information about financial statements. Like the national economic reports, the listed companies' financial statements are described as long and complicated because of the extensive data they contain regarding companies' economic conditions. The investors explain that the TV news only reports whether the company has deficits or earnings. Compared to non-ICT users, who can only obtain incomplete financial statements from practices like watching TV, ICT users can check for the full reports online.

Aside from ICT usage, another factor that stands out regarding communicating financial statements is expertise. For example, the small investor Ms. Li worried that she might miss some data contained in the reports, but she also mentioned that "it is more important" to make sense of the financial statements professionally, in essence, to distinguish between bull news or bear news:

> Even if I can read the full reports online, I can't understand them. I do not understand the complicated data. I do not have the professional knowledge to do so. I just want to know whether the statement is bull or bear news. The stock commentators will say if the company has earned or lost money recently.

At this point, it seems the professional have-mores and ICT users have the upper hand in communicating companies' financial statements. Those who either lack digital devices or expertise in reading financial statements evaluate their practices as unsatisfactory and risky, a situation made worse by the fact that someone else could react faster and more accurately; thus, they cannot trade the stocks at their desired price. A practice-shifting moment happens here: The non-ICT users withdraw from the position of competitor with other investors. Instead, they position themselves as the information acquirer and turn to the experts for help. To hand over the risk communicator position is to partially hand over autonomy in stock investment, which means they become the underdog in the whole risk communication chain for company financial statements.

But is ICT and expertise enough for some investors to feel secure in their advantaged position? Interestingly, in the interviews, the individual investors who use ICT complained that they are almost "overwhelmed" (in the words of Mr. Qin and Mr. Huang) by the information contained in companies' financial statements. Huang outlined why he sees risk in communicating financial statements: "There used to be eight listed companies on the market. But now there are thousands. How could I possibly get to know them all?" From a communication research angle, there is a relevant theory here called the knowledge gap (Tichenor, Donohue, & Olien, 1970; Donohue, Tichenor, & Olien, 1975). This theory assumes that higher socioeconomic individuals acquire information quicker than people in lower strata, thus causing the information gap between social groups to grow. The issue with communicating financial statements in China goes beyond the knowledge gap theory: No matter how professional a person is, he or she cannot deal with the digital information explosion in financial statements, simply because of the energy limitations of human beings. For example, Mr. Zeng, a junior analyst, told me that "it's impossible" to absorb the financial statements without teamwork at his company. Xia, a college student with no team to depend on, admits that he's struggling between his grade point average and company analyses:

> I almost failed two courses last semester—don't get me wrong, they are not financial courses. I always get high scores in financial courses. Stock investment just takes up too much of my time. I am so torn. My dream (graduate) school requires a very high GPA.

He stared at his stock investment app while talking, and then fell into a long silence.

At this point, it seems quite obvious that finance companies and their representatives are the most vocal and convincing communicators of financial statements. They have digital devices, expertise, and human resources all at hand. And, there seems to be no reason for individuals to insist on stock trading on their own, taking on huge risk that they could hand over to institutions. Why do the individual investors, most of whom are small investors, resist taking themselves out of the risk communication process with company financial statements? One of the most crucial reasons for this choice is that Chinese investors distrust the financial statements of listed companies. They question the honesty of the executive officers and accounting firms who publicize information. Numerous scandals, lawsuits, and government penalties seem to legitimate this concern—and that's not even mentioning the many suspicious cases not officially under investigation. For example, the 530 crisis mentioned in the last chapter has left an ugly scar on the trust between the investors and the government. Similarly, a crisis at a listed company also plays an important role in corroding the happy relations between investors and companies. In 2001, a magazine named *Caijing* published an article called "The Yin (Chuan) Guangxia Trap,"[1] which caused a storm in China's financial markets. To illustrate the hidden risk of that trap, the magazine cover showed a faceless figure with shark teeth wearing a hoodie and a hat with Guangxia's company icon. The journalists accused the Yinchuan Guangxia Industrial Corporation, a rising star in China's stock markets, of faking the profits and performance stats in its financial statements. Experts found the company's claims regarding its extraction services to be simply impossible. Meanwhile, the company's reported profits from exporting products to Germany were ridiculous when considering the standardized global price—56.10 and 180 million Deutsche Mark (about 30 million and 84 million USD at that time) in 1999 and 2000, respectively. The journalists went to Zhongtianqin, a once leading accounting firm that audited the financial statements of Yinchuan Guangxia, asking for more detailed documents. The firm cooperated, handing over the documents (which, from a professional point of view, was strange enough). The company asserted that it did the auditing job based upon the data submitted by Yinchuan Guangxia, without double-checking with the government bureau. According to the journalists, this excuse failed to explain the fact that the serial numbers on many export declaration forms were missing. How could the accountants ignore these blanks? The Bureau of Tianjin Port, on the other hand, told the journalists a very different story of the company's exports: In 1999, the exports were 4,819,272 US dollars, while in 2000, they were only 33,571 US dollars. These numbers were extremely far removed from the 30 million and 84 million US dollars claimed. The journalists ended the article with this statement:

> The whole thing—from large extraction products exports, to the sudden surge in Yin(chuan) Guanxia's profits, to the ridiculous increase in the stock price—is totally a fraud. We journalists still remember the day that we eventually got (our assumption) confirmed by the Tianjin Port Bureau. The sunshine in July was dazzling and bright. Under the bright light, we seemed to hear a crispy sound indicating that the bubble has burst. Finally, we know the truth, it's simple and cruel.

Despite the "simple and cruel" truth about the financial statements of Yin Guangxia, journalists had questioned the ballooning of the stock price *before* the release of the polished financial statements. From December 30, 1999 to April 19, 2000, the price dramatically increased from 13.97 to 35.83. According to *Caijing*, all of these signs pointed to a trap targeting investors, a possibility that someone was purposely manipulating the market through insider information. On August 2 and 3, 2001, multiple web portals cited "The Yin (Chuan) Guangxia Trap," immediately triggering market panic. Yin Guangxia launched an emergency board meeting and soon applied to suspend its security trading on the Shenzhen Stock Market in early August, saying in its announcement:

> On the nights of August 2 and 3, some media outlets published a news article about our company. The publishing of this article could possibly lead to abnormal fluctuation of the stock prices, and to protect the interest of investors, our company … has applied for emergency suspension of stock trading.[2]

In its announcement, the company did not deny, even slightly, the accusations published in *Caijing*, confirming the suspicions directed toward them. The China Securities Regulatory Commission (CSRC) stepped in soon after the article was published, investigating in the company's financial condition. Xinhua News Agency, the dominant state-owned news agency in China, reported that the CSRC had formed an investigation team, who had done fieldwork in Yinchuan, Shenzhen, Shanghai, Wuhu, and Wuhan to thoroughly investigate the case of Yin Guangxia, eventually concluding that the company "was bold as hell," doing the dirty work to polish their financial statements "by hook or by crook."[3] The company's financial department admitted that it had started to fake its economic conditions in 1995. Shockingly, the stock became tradable again in September, triggering huge debates on whether the government should simply delist such problematic companies from the market.[4] Immediately after the stock started trading, the company's price crashed, and small investors mourned. Eventually, several executive officers from the company ended up in prison, and the once leading accounting firm that generated the financial statements for YingGuangxia, Zhongtianqin, had its license revoked. The YingGuangxia Cooperation and Zhongtianqin firm case may be considered the Chinese version of the Enron and Arthur Andersen scandal in the United States, which happened the same year.[5] Enron Corporation was once a blossoming company in the energy industry, but after being involved in multiple cases of fraudulent financial statements and insider trading scandals, it ended up in bankruptcy. As for Arthur Andersen, the once leading figure in audit and accountancy partnership, he surrendered his license as Enron auditor. Due to the numerous similarities between these cases, financial researchers tend to mention them together when analyzing financial scandals, especially accounting fraud (e.g. Alles, Kogan, & Vasarhelyi, 2002; Joshi et al., 2007; Firth, Mo, & Wong, 2014).

The difference between the two cases is that the Enron crisis did not permanently destabilize the expert-oriented risk culture of the United States' financial world. Suspicion of course exists, but overall, people regained trust in financial statements, especially after the release of Sarbanes–Oxley Act[6] in 2002, which tightened the auditing procedures of listed companies.[7] But in China, it wasn't until 2004 that the Securities Laws (published in 1998) were officially revised, and investors still question the pressure that the government puts on listed companies and accounting firms. To be fair, even when the government takes action and launches company investigations, the investors become more convinced of their stance: "You see? There could be more."

This belief is shared by both the professionals and nonprofessionals, the rich and the poor. For example, Ms. Yu, a senior analyst, told me, "What I worry about is whether the financial statements reflect the true conditions of the companies or not. Some of them (the companies) cheat on their financial statements. It's not a secret." She mentioned that she sometimes takes a closer look at the accounting firms that conduct the companies' audits because she knows that "some generally follow the rules, and some are not decent by any means." Mr. Liang, a professional investor seeking a "solution" to gain more solid company news, also uses his guanxi to verify companies' financial statements.

To be frank, I wouldn't touch those companies that neither I nor my colleagues or my friends are familiar with. No matter how wonderful the performance (of the company) looks. Sometimes, the more polished it looks, the more dangers are hidden behind it. It's China's stock market. Don't forget that. The risk is too high.

Because "the risk is too high" to rely on the normal way of communicating financial statements, a practice-shifting moment happens for big investors, one in which they privately shift to their guanxi in order to obtain or verify information about the listed companies. In this instance, they rely on this practice more than their professional experience in examining published financial statements. Mr. Chen, who told me the "story" of big banker X, said angrily,

> If every financial statement were generated with honesty, I, as a professional analyst, certainly could explain it efficiently and predict the future tendencies of the company with the help of past financial statements and other public information. But they are not (generated with honesty). My profession is useless.

When the big investors have to position themselves as inquirers of insider information instead of professional analysts, on the one hand, they hold a privileged position in risk communication because they can evaluate the risk of a company more accurately than small investors. On the other hand, however, the risk in such communication processes bothers big investors. While positioning themselves as professional analysts, they have their own knowledge as a foundation; they have no need to ask others for help. However, when positioning themselves as insider information inquirers, they hold a lower position than the sharers, requiring them to ask for "big favors" while hoping for an answer. Then, of course, there is the pressure from law enforcement.

Then what about the sanhu (small investors) in China? Are they naïve followers of financial statements, or do they keep a cautious eye on the risk definition of listed companies generated by the social expert system? All the small investors interviewed for this book are fully aware of the risk in financial statement communication, due to all the "lessens" they have learned from scandals like Yin Guangxia case. The major risk for small investors comes from the untrustworthiness of financial statements. Mr. Qin, a small investor who's always critical of government authorities, points a finger at the listed companies, the accounting firms, and the government:

> I think some companies give bribes to the accounting firms to fake financial statements. Indeed, I think some of the listed companies are not qualified enough to be in the market. I think the government should do more to kick them out.

What makes the situation even worse is the exchange of insider information between the big bankers and the companies. Ms. Li, a small investor, stated, "Some companies leak information to the big investors. They (the big investors) set everything up in advance, and the small investors have to buy the stocks for a higher price or sell the stocks for a lower price." Li and other small investors face inequality in their trading practices in terms of the timing of obtaining financial statements. When evaluating the trading practice after obtaining financial statements, the investors construct zero-sum relations between the big and small investors because the quicker reactions of the big investors are perceived as a risk to the small investors; thus, the small investors are not always able to buy or sell stocks at decent prices.

Unlike the big investors, the small investors rarely have the guanxi to gain security in communicating financial statements. Let's look back at how the big investors develop guanxi. Basically, obtaining a "big favor" in guanxi requires both a trusting relationship and the ability to return a big favor. Ms. Yu's judgment of the accounting firms, for example, comes from her guanxi with her classmates from a top university who later went to work in the fields of accounting and auditing. She will casually give her classmates "professional stock investment advice" but "in an absolutely legal way." By comparison, big banker X's guanxi with listed companies is purely based upon illegal bribery, according to Mr. Chen.

Because the majority of small investors are not able to build up such guanxi, they deal with listed companies' financial statements in their own ways, using their ICT devices. First of all, ignoring the government's warnings about the risk of excessive speculation, they insist on speculating on stocks, instead of investing in a listed company for the long term. The investors explain that they have little faith in the long-term running of the companies. A very positive financial statement is regarded as big bull news, and they do not want to put money in the stock market for a long term. For example, Mr. Zhang, a small investor, told me, "Problems with the company will eventually come up. They fake it (the financial statement) once, twice, but not forever. I need to withdraw (my money) from (the stocks) before the economic problems of the company come out." The securities firms and the whole electronic trading system mentioned in Chapter 3 support such behaviors. And this is one of the major reasons that the small investors do not want to entrust the fund managers to deal with their financial investments: The withdrawing of money from a fund is usually not as easy and quick.

But to manage their own investments, the small investors face an overwhelming number of financial statements on their own. Even though they do not believe these statements, they still consider them to be important references. Without institutional backup, small investors typically deal with such issues by narrowing down their portfolios to a handful of companies. The college student Xia showed me how he put nine companies into his "favorite folder" using stock software. It's also common for some individual investors (e.g. Huang and Li) to focus only on one or two companies at a time—which would make an expert frown because there is no way for them to reduce the unsystematic risk through diversification of portfolio.[8] However, the strategy of the small investors to focus on a small number of public companies does not reflect the irrationality of them. Rather, they have evaluated the risk in communicating financial statements carefully, reaching the conclusion that risk in entrusting an institution to deal with their investments is too high. They therefore stick with their own apps and software. Meanwhile, they even seek insider information and stock commentary online, a topic that will be examined in the next chapter. As Mr. Huang, a small investor, puts it, "I know it's (a piece of insider information about a company) probably unreliable. But the financial statements are also unreliable. Why not take a shot?"

And are nonofficial Internet sources completely unreliable? To answer this question, we have to revisit a media report about the Yin Guangxia scandal entitled, "The Yin (Chuan) Guangxia Trap." In the article, the journalists wrote the following:

> Within the industry of security investment, few people bought the story of the Yin Guangxia Miracle. A fund manager said, 'It (the performance of Yin Guangxia) is good; however, it is not consistent with normality.' Another famous researcher of a brokerage firm did not include Yin Guangxia on his observations list. We asked him why, and his answer was, 'Is it necessary to investigate it?' ... People discussed Yin Guangxia on various financial websites, with very different points of view. On a famous online forum for stock discussion, 'Hexun, Let's Discuss Together,' there were thousands of posts about Yin Guangxia, with supporters and opponents holding very different positions, continuously arguing with each other. We can see the abundance of hearsay there.

The first part of the journalists' observation referred to the experts' understanding of financial statements. The fund managers and stock analysts in the article, like Ms. Yu and Mr. Liang, were very tuned in to the internal controversies regarding the company's condition, as only an expert can tell. We can assume that big investors, especially institutional ones with an expert team on their side, are all aware of the uncertainties inherent in China's auditing process. Even if the big investors do not see anything suspicious in the financial statements, they may be able to tell that something is wrong through their money-developed guanxi networks with accounting firms, law firms, listed company executives, and corrupt government officials. In contrast, the small investors, who are believed to be professional have-lesses, are apparently less capable of finding the devil in the details (of course, some of them have tried their best to learn about the finance industry), nor do they have the capital to develop guanxi and gain valuable insider information. Facing this disadvantage, some small investors, like netizens in the Hexun forums, used the Internet as an information source to catch up with the experts/big investors. In the Yin Guangxia scandal, it is clear that Internet sources were more unstable and less reliable than the experts' sources with regard to the true conditions of Yin Guangxia. Questionable gossip was communicated on the forums. As the journalists mentioned, there were fierce supporters of Yin Guangxia, and their online discourse might have misled investors with a neutral position. But at least cyberspace has brought the topic of suspicious company statuses to the table for discussion and questioning, exposing problematic financial conditions to the online public. Compared with the cyber debates on Yin Guangxia, the traditional mass media treated the company extremely well, keeping comparatively silent about the suspicious parts of the company's information. A search using the key word "Yin Guangxia" on WiseNews, the Chinese newspaper and magazine database, shows that the majority of the news articles published from 1999 to early 2001 from major media outlets admired the company's boom using an optimistic tone. Doubts only gradually emerge after the first season of 2001. The overall media image of Yin Guangxia was extremely positive in 1999 and 2000. The media portrayed the company as a caring, responsible, and high-tech rising star in China. If we revisit these news articles, we can see that the company (probably on purpose) catered to national policy in order to promote itself. In early 2000, the Communist Party launched China's Western Development Program, aiming to largely improve the infrastructure, educational system, and economic status of China's western provinces. Yin Guangxia, despite its major business claim of being in the extraction and exports business, soon started an afforestation project in the western part of China. Such activities certainly caught the attention of the mainstream media. *People's Daily*, the mouthpiece of Communist Party, praised Yin Guangxia by describing its environmental project in the desert as "a miracle." In one of its article published on September 19, 2000, the paper stated, "Yin Guangxia is a listed company, and it is of course seeking profits. But the great thing about this company is that it has combined economic gains and ecological results, making profits while protecting the ecological system." We can somehow understand such positive comments from *People's Daily*, because it discusses Yin Guangxia from the point of view of a supporter of national policies, instead of as a financial expert. It is, however, interesting to see that the dominant newspapers in finance also consistently drew a beautiful picture when communicating Yin Guangxia's company information. *Shanghai Securities News*, for example, mentioned to its readers that

Yin Guangxia's extraction service (which, as discussed above, was a total fraud) had reached the level of having "one of the most advanced extraction technologies in the world." Even when the voices that challenged Yin Guangxia emerged, another influential media outlet, *Market Guide News*, published an article called "Yin Guangxia, Growing with Debates," saying,

> Through the research on Yin Guangxia, (we) have found that this company is indeed debatable in many aspects, but if we take a deep study of the company, we can find some positives as well ... It has garnered great public approval, not just because it is packaged well.

If journalists were deceived by the polished financial statements, it is astonishing that the experts did not express any reservations. They kept silent in their research reports for quite some time. In 2010, when *Shanghai Securities News* published a retrospective article about the Yin Guangxia case called "Farewell, Yin Guangxia Trap," the journalists wrote, "From 1999 to 2001, relevant research institutions at brokerages published many research articles about Yin Guangxia. Some of the people who drafted the reports were researchers from big brokerages. Not a single report challenged Yin Guangxia's performance." Among all of the media reports from 1999 to 2001, one of the very few articles "badmouthing" Yin Guangxia published in the mass media was a letter from a reader in the *China Securities Journal*. This reader expressed his doubts about the polished yet confusing financial statements. The author of this letter was a retired university teacher who had taught himself about the stock market; he was not even a financial expert. Clearly, though many experts frowned at Yin Guangxia's company news and financial statements in their boardrooms, the majority was reluctant to openly question the company. A senior financial analyst who experienced the Yin Guangxia scandal period explained the unusual reaction of experts to me:

> First of all, to my memory, it was unfair to call (the expert community's critiques of Yin Guangxia) a complete silence. I do remember some experts pointing a finger at the company. And you can't really blame these funds managers and analysts (who did not express their doubts about Yin Guangxia). We need hard evidence (demonstrating that the financial statements are false), or we will be sued. A doubt is a doubt. Openly saying a financial statement is problematic requires more than a simple statement. Apart from this concern, you don't know who's behind these public companies. What if they have very strong guanxi? Why risk the finance companies' fame to do that? We just put together a decent portfolio for our customers, because there are other choices on the market. That's the right way for experts to

earn money in China. And to be honest, at that time, the market lacked 'tools' for short sellers. In the oversea markets, short sellers can earn a lot.[9] Not in China, though, especially in Yin Guangxia's time period. No interest, no driving force. (The situation) might change if we had more short-selling tools in China's market though.

In this chapter, I have mentioned the "devaluation" of publicly communicated company news, and, in this analyst's declaration, we can see the specter of devaluation overshadowing the communication of financial statements as well. In many cases, the expert system is reluctant to provide critical risk evaluations of listed companies for the government or for the public, simply because the uncertainty of their own guanxi is so high and the chance of profits so extremely low. They also worry that any "radical" negative comments could upset the small investors who have invested in the targeted stock. Nonetheless, it's very common for the global finance companies to release aggressive interpretations of financial statements to demonstrate their own risk definition ability in finance, thus attracting more customers. Compared to their Western peers, the Chinese experts are trapped in a paradox: They need to demonstrate their ability to communicate company information, yet their professionalism has to be invoked in a distorted way in public to avoid risk to themselves. (But indeed, how can they claim to practice their true ability in private while winning the trust of the public?) The "cooked" company information from finance companies publicized on traditional and new media—from reports on financial statements and comments on company news—is no longer that valuable. None of this discourse reflects the real thoughts expressed in board rooms about public companies.

The small investors have witnessed the devaluation of public information lesson by lesson, including the Yin Guangxia crisis. They thus have turned to the Internet for help. Based on the evidence, we can conclude that, without online debate about Yin Guangxia, the company's deception might have duped even more small investors before *Caijing* exposed its true nature. According to the World Bank,[10] in 1999, only 0.708% of China's population had Internet access, a percentage that reached 2.64% in 2001. This number has grown rapidly but still remains comparatively low. Only a small portion of small investors were Internet users who would have seen the online posts expressing doubts about Yin Guangxia. In 2016, over 50% of Chinese people were able to surf the Internet using different digital devices. The population of small investors today who can access alternative (but to be fair, not necessarily true) interpretations of company information has increased tremendously. Those who doubt a company's official risk definition or evaluation now have a convenient and inexpensive channel to express their opinions. A critical researcher may observe such phenomena with great interest, especially given that netizens in China are known to launch powerful protests addressing various social problems (e.g. Herold, 2008; Yang, 2009, 2011; Qiang, 2011). Though hampered by cyber censorship, netizens' online protests have removed several corrupt politicians and bureaucrats from their positions (Montgomery, Shen, & Chen, 2014; Tai, 2015; Gorman, 2016; Zhang et al., 2017). They also have delivered multiple blows to companies they believe to be problematic (Yang, 2010; Cao, 2015; Jian & Chan, 2016). During critical moments, cyberspace can reversely influence the agenda setting and framing strategy of mass media, persuading more conservative outlets to address critical social issues that were once silenced or ignored, eventually forcing the political regime to respond to the public call (Zhou & Moy, 2007; Jiang, 2014). Regarding the communication of company information, is it possible that the general public, having lost trust and patience in the official expert system, has seized an important role through digital media? Are they challenging or even taking over the supervisor position from the political regime and mass media? Are they taking control of the risk evaluator position from the listed companies and accounting firms?

Seeing netizens' enthusiastic discussions about listed companies, the answer is a self-evident yes. But what we cannot neglect is the nature of online discourse, which is both rebellious and disorganized. The information online tends to be scattered, sometimes baseless and misleading, if not a complete lie. Only a few cases mediated on the online forums and social media have managed to catch the attention of the traditional media and political regime. And it is this attention that has played the most important role in the fate of listed companies from the 2001 Ying Guangxia scandal to present. The remaining questions and suspicions easily can be ignored as gossip and hearsay. Meanwhile, digital media has leveled the playing field by reducing the cost of mass communication for a critical netizen with a piece of interesting company information.

However, it also has opened the floodgates for blackmailers and manipulators. On the afternoon of April 26, 2018, a piece of company information burst onto the scene, appearing on several of China's social media platforms: The giant insurance company Ping An Insurance[11] would change its chairman of the board. It was close to the time when Ping An Insurance released its financial statement—which indeed seemed impressive, showing a very strongly performing company. At the same time, such a major internal change clearly indicates some sort of instability in the company. The market panicked as people quickly began reposting the information online. Ping An Insurance immediately reacted through its official social media account, saying that the rumors about a change in chairman were completely false. The company threatened to contact the police regarding the fraud; however, this declaration was reposted less than 100 times,[12] far less distributed than the original gossip. Some of those who reposted Ping An Insurance's microblog expressed distrust toward the company: "You are so done." "Ping An said it's a rumor. We will just wait and see the change (or chairman)." Between the shining financial statement from officials and an untraceable story from out of nowhere attacking the company, many Chinese investors surprisingly believed the rumors without hesitation. The stock price of Ping An Insurance decreased dramatically after the rumor began circulating, dealing a huge blow to the company and its investors.[13] Digital media thus has become a double-edged sword in people's communication of company news. Only looking at the bright side or the dark side of these newly emerged platforms would oversimplify the complicated nature of financial communication in China. This dualism also exists when people communicate stock commentary, a topic that I will explore further in the next chapter.

Notes

1 The original news article is available at: http://magazine.caijing.com.cn/20010805/111291.shtml
2 See the original announcement here: http://finance.sina.com.cn/stock/company/sz/000557/24/32.shtml
3 See the original report here: http://www.people.com.cn/GB/jinji/20020527/737575.html
4 Some media criticized that Yin Guangxia should be delisted according to China's Company Law. They argued that the company was not removed from the market only to protect the interests of the "bankers", to win them some time to sell out the securities (see http://finance.sina.com.cn/t/20010915/107688.html). The readers can read Chapter 2 for more details about IPO and delisting issue on China's financial market.
5 For more details about Enron scandal, see Nelson, Price and Rountree (2008), Asthana, Balsam, and Kim, (2009), and Sridharan, Caines, McMillan, and Summers (2002).
6 The full text of the Sarbanes-Oxley Act is available at: http://legcounsel.house.gov/Comps/Sarbanes-oxley%20Act%20Of%202002.pdf
7 For more details about Sarbanes-Oxley Act, its explanations, and possible consequences on United States' financial market, see the research of Hoitash, Hoitash, and Bedard (2008), Coates and John (2007), and Ge and Mcvay (2005). The readers can also read *What is Sarbanes-Oxley?* By Guy Lander or *Manager's guide to the Sarbanes-Oxley Act: Improving internal controls to prevent fraud* by Scott Green to see the thoughts from the industry about the Act.
8 Unsystematic risk is also known "specific risk," which refers to the uncertainties toward specific asset or company (for example, a piece of negative company news). Some financial researchers believe that such kind of risk can be reduced through diversification of portfolio, AKA investing in various companies. The diversified portfolio, however, cannot reduce systematic risk or so-called market risk, which refers to the risk inherent to the entire market (e.g. currency crisis, national-leveled catastrophes). For more information about unsystematic risk and systematic risk, readers can have

a look at Markowitz's (1952, 1991, & 1999) classic portfolio theory and some follow-up research on the issue of unsystematic risk, systematic risk, and diversification of portfolio (e.g. Wagner & Law, 1971; Statman, 1987; Lubatkin & Chatterjee, 1994).

9 A typical short selling action occurred in May 2018. A short seller called Blue Orca Capital hit Samsonite International SA, one of the world's largest luggage manufacturers and retailers that was going public on Hong Kong stock market. Blue Orca Capital released an online report (data available at https://www.blueorcacapital.com/) questioning the company's performance and its strategy to conceal its real performance. In addition, the company's CEO, Ramesh Tainwala, had committed fraud on his resume by claiming to be a doctor. On its public Twitter account, Blue Orca Capital claimed, "Blue Orca is Short Samsonite (HK: 1910), which we value at HKD 17.59 per share, 48% below Samsonite's last traded price" (See https://twitter.com/blueorcainvest/status/999480338123513856). The stock prices of Samsonite plummeted after the report was released, and Ramesh Tainwala resigned from the company days after the fraudulent resume accusation (see the news reports   https://www.bloomberg.com/news/articles/2018-05-31/samsonite-ceo-resigns-as-short-seller-charges-jolt-luggage-firm and https://www.nytimes.com/2018/06/01/business/samsonite-chief-resign.html for reference).

10 The data can be retrieved at: https://data.worldbank.org/indicator/IT.NET.USER.ZS?locations=CN&name_desc=false

11 Read the information on Ping An Insurance's official website for more details about the company: http://www.pingan.cn/en/index.shtml

12 See the ordinal Weibo post here: https://weibo.com/1650507560/GdSYlncQr

13 On 26 April 2018, Ping An Insurance's stock price dropped over 3% on China's stock market, and on April 27, 2018, it's price kept dropping about 5%, and only at the end of the trading hours it slightly bounced back. Ping An Insurance's stock price in the Hong Kong stock market also plummeted dramatically. Even Ping An Bank Co., Ltd., another listed company under Ping An Group, suffered crash in stock prices due to the online rumor.

References

Alles, M. G., Kogan, A., & Vasarhelyi, M. A. (2002). *Lessons for China from the crisis in US auditing continuous assurance, mandatory auditor rotation, separating auditing from consulting and tertiary logging.* Paper for the 4th Asia-Pacific Journal of Accounting and Economics Symposium Shanghai, the People's Republic of China, January 2003.

Asthana, S., Balsam, S., & Kim, S. (2009). The effect of Enron, Andersen, and Sarbanes-Oxley on the US market for audit services. *Accounting Research Journal*, 22(1), 4–26.

Cao, D. (2015). *Animals in China*. London: Palgrave Macmillan.

Coates, I. V., & John, C. (2007). The goals and promise of the Sarbanes-Oxley Act. *Journal of Economic Perspectives*, 21(1), 91–116.

Donohue, G. A., Tichenor, P. J., & Olien, C. N. (1975). Mass media and the knowledge gap: A hypothesis reconsidered. *Communication Research*, 2(1), 3–23.

Firth, M. A., Mo, P. L. L., & Wong, R. M. (2014). Auditors' reporting conservatism after regulatory sanctions: Evidence from China. *Journal of International Accounting Research*, 13(2), 1–24.

Ge, W., & McVay, S. (2005). The disclosure of material weaknesses in internal control after the Sarbanes-Oxley Act. *Accounting Horizons, 19*(3), 137–158.

Gorman, P. (2016). Flesh searches in China: The governmentality of online engagement and media management. *Asian Survey, 56*(2), 325–347.

Green, S. (2004). *Manager's guide to the Sarbanes-Oxley Act: Improving internal controls to prevent fraud.* New York: John Wiley & Sons.

Herold, D. K. (2008). Development of a civic society online? Internet vigilantism and state control in Chinese cyberspace. *Asia Journal of Global Studies, 2*(1), 26–37.

Hoitash, R., Hoitash, U., & Bedard, J. C. (2008). Internal control quality and audit pricing under the Sarbanes-Oxley Act. *Auditing: A Journal of Practice & Theory, 27*(1), 105–126.

Jian, L., & Chan, C. K. C. (2016). Collective identity, framing and mobilisation of environmental protests in urban China: A case study of Qidong's protest. *China: An International Journal, 14*(2), 102–122.

Jiang, Y. (2014). "Reversed agenda-setting effects" in China Case studies of Weibo trending topics and the effects on state-owned media in China. *Journal of International Communication, 20*(2), 168–183.

Joshi, P. L., Bremser, W. G., Hemalatha, J., & Al-Mudhaki, J. (2007). Non-audit services and auditor independence: Empirical findings from Bahrain. *International Journal of Accounting, Auditing and Performance Evaluation, 4*(1), 57–89.

Lander, G. P. (2004). *What is Sarbanes-Oxley?* New York: McGraw Hill.

Lubatkin, M., & Chatterjee, S. (1994). Extending modern portfolio theory into the domain of corporate diversification: Does it apply? *Academy of Management Journal, 37*(1), 109–136.

Markowitz, H. (1952). Portfolio selection. *The Journal of Finance, 7*(1), 77–91.

Markowitz, H. M. (1991). Foundations of portfolio theory. *The Journal of Finance, 46*(2), 469–477.

Markowitz, H. M. (1999). The early history of portfolio theory: 1600–1960. *Financial Analysts Journal, 55*(4), 5–16.

Montgomery, M., Shen, J., & Chen, T. (2014, December). Digital discourse and changing forms of political engagement: A case study of two separate episodes in contrasting mediaspheres—"Binders full of women" in the US and "Watchgate" in the PRC. In *Electronic Proceedings* (p. 160). Brussels, Belgium.

Nelson, K. K., Price, R. A., & Rountree, B. R. (2008). The market reaction to Arthur Andersen's role in the Enron scandal: Loss of reputation or confounding effects? *Journal of Accounting and Economics, 46*(2–3), 279–293.

Qiang, X. (2011). The battle for the Chinese Internet. *Journal of Democracy, 22*(2), 47–61.

Rong, Y., Xu, E., & Li, N. (2015, August). Mining a microblog network on anti-corruption news with Social Network Analysis. In *2015 12th International Conference on Fuzzy Systems and Knowledge Discovery (FSKD) 2015* (pp. 1432–1436). IEEE.

Sridharan, U. V., Caines, W. R., McMillan, J., & Summers, S. (2002). Financial statement transparency and auditor responsibility: Enron and Andersen. *International Journal of Auditing, 6*(3), 277–286.

Statman, M. (1987). How many stocks make a diversified portfolio? *Journal of Financial and Quantitative Analysis, 22*(3), 353–363.

Tai, Z. (2015). Networked resistance: Digital populism, online activism, and mass dissent in China. *Popular Communication, 13*(2), 120–131.

Tichenor, P. J., Donohue, G. A., & Olien, C. N. (1970). Mass media flow and differential growth in knowledge. *Public Opinion Quarterly, 34*(2), 159–170.

Wagner, W. H., & Lau, S. C. (1971). The effect of diversification on risk. *Financial Analysts Journal, 27*(6), 48–53.

Yang, G. (2009). *The power of the Internet in China: Citizen activism online.* New York: Columbia University Press.

Yang, G. (2010). Brokering environment and health in China: Issue entrepreneurs of the public sphere. *Journal of Contemporary China, 19*(63), 101–118.

Yang, G. (2011). Technology and its contents: Issues in the study of the Chinese Internet. *The Journal of Asian Studies, 70*(4), 1043–1050.

Zhang, W., Cui, P., Wang, T., & Wen, J. (2017). Dynamic evolutionary analysis of government's response capacity to public emergencies. *Journal of Computational and Theoretical Nanoscience, 14*(1), 137–145.

Zhou, Y., & Moy, P. (2007). Parsing framing processes: The interplay between online public opinion and media coverage. *Journal of Communication, 57*(1), 79–98.

6 Stock Commentators and Commentary

From the former chapters, the readers may have gained an understanding of the important players and their roles in communicating different financial information in China, including small investors, big investors, government authorities, companies, accounting firms, brokerages, and some individual experts. Sometimes competing and sometimes cooperating, they all seek to seize dominant positions as risk definers in the financial world—even at the expense of other players. Though underdogs, the small investors keep themselves on the field through information and communication technologies (ICTs), criticizing, evaluating, asking questions, and exchanging ideas about financial risk. Interestingly, much of the information we have seen is raw, meaning it must be transformed into directional messages that guide people's trading practices. But what happens with the communication of "more valuable" information, information that has already been verified or analyzed? In the previous chapter, I mentioned one type of such information, known as insider information (*neimuxiaoxi*). In this chapter, I would like to discuss two other types of "cooked" information, namely stock commentary (*guping*) and stock opinions (*kanfa*). The communication of these two types of information greatly influences the risk culture in China, and once again, digital media technologies play an important role in this communication process, especially in reconstructing the meanings of the profession.

Stock Commentary and Commentators

Stock commentary (*guping*) provides information based on stock market analysis. This information is shared publicly through TV, radio, newspapers, and digital media by professional have-mores, known as stock commentators (*gupingjia*). Based on the data, we can conclude that investors in China only consider a piece of information to be stock commentary when it satisfies the above definition. The definitions are fixed when it comes to who shares information (stock commentators), what kind of information they share (explanations and predictions about stocks), and the way they share it (publicly).

Not all professional have-mores choose to become stock commentators. Ms. Yu, for example, didn't like the idea of sharing her stock analysis publicly. "It's a bit bizarre to me," said Ms. Yu, "I prefer to share information with my customers in person." However, some people do not mind being watched and listened to by the public. Of all the interviewed stock commentators, I chose the three most interesting to share with the readers. Among these three commentators, we have a junior analyst, Mr. Zeng, who works for a consulting firm and usually shares his stock commentary in newspapers, magazines, blogs, and microblogs. The other two are senior analysts. Mr. Gao, who now works as a senior financial analyst for a stock company, used to be a very active stock commentator. He has been invited by several newspapers to write columns and by some TV programs to share his stock commentary. He still provides stock commentary on his stock company website, but he avoids exposure on the highly public stage. Finally, Mr. Liang is slightly younger than Mr. Gao, but has nearly the same amount of experience in the stock market. He currently is a stock commentator representing his finance company, and he usually shares his stock commentary in newspapers and on his blog. He also has been on a number of TV and radio programs. Zeng and Liang invest in stocks personally aside from their institutional activities, but they declare that their investing practices are legal because they would not touch the listed companies that have a business relationship with their institutions.

When I interviewed different stock commentators, whether senior or rookie, I was first curious about what makes a stock commentator a stock commentator. They generally note that today in China, a stock commentator must have official certificates such as the Certification of Securities Professional (Securities Association of China, 2014) or the Professional Certificate of Security Investment Consulting (China Securities Regulatory Commission, 2014). Mr. Zeng said that some pirate radio shows invite unlicensed stock commentators to share their analysis, but "overall, this phenomenon is seen less and less." Zeng and some professional have-lesses, such as Ms. Li, suggested that the official certifications indicate authority, expertise, and reliability. For example, Li stated, "I heard they (the certificate owners) need to pass many exams. Their expertise has been tested. I trust those with these certifications more. At least they are licensed, not unlicensed (*yeluzi*)." Some financial TV programs even show the serial number of the stock commentators' professional certification to assure the audience. A stock commentator may become a risk definer in finance, with his or her expertise as a weapon. Therefore, the government authorities use this license to define the expertise and the expert, the process of which allows the government to become the ultimate ruler of risk communication in the market.

But only having the license is not enough to be a "recognized" stock commentator, as can be seen in the life story of Mr. Zeng, who told me about his career path.

After I graduated from the department of finance with a master's degree, I got a job in the finance industry. The finance companies in China encourage their consultants and analysts to work as stock commentators in the media, to promote the reputation of the firm. In order to become a stock commentator, I worked hard to pass different exams to gain the certificates, which are proof that you have a certain level of professional knowledge. But, they (the certificates) do not mean that you can be a stock commentator. You have to share decent analyses consistently when doing your job and build up your reputation among the professionals before managers will recommend you to newspaper editors or TV producers. I am very lucky to write stock commentary for several very decent newspapers. When you are invited by the newspapers, TV programs, or radio stations to share your opinions, it means you are a stock commentator. People listen to your stock commentary. People follow you.

According to Mr. Zeng, a professional background in finance and government certifications are just the "basic requirements" of a stock commentator. Nowadays, another two "definers of risk definers" stand out due to their control over stock commentary. First of all, the financial service companies (e.g. a brokerage, a fund, an investing bank, a consulting company) are supposed to recommend the best of the best to the mass media, representing the company in public in order to attract more customers. The mass media, on the other hand, recruit licensed guests from the finance companies or from the market directly. These two institutions serve as the gatekeepers of stock commentary, supposedly ensuring the quality of the professional's educational background, certificates, experience, and reputation as a vocal risk definer. They represent restricted access that "not everyone can be a fund manager ... or write a column for the decent newspaper" (Ms. Li).

On the contrary, digital media is famous for their "affordances," which facilitate individual communicators to express their own voices inexpensively (e.g. Dominick, 2010). Regarding financial risk, however, such easy access seems to reduce the reliability and value of their voices. Though every investor is able to express their opinions online, those opinions are not viewed as stock commentary and barely get communicated. Indeed, Xia, a college student who wrote a microblog about the Everbright crisis mentioned in Chapter 1, only received three retweets and nine likes. Ostensibly, the online sphere has just become another stage for the stock commentators to promote themselves and act as opinion leaders in financial communication. In personal profiles on his blog and microblog, Mr. Zeng proudly mentioned that he is a stock commentator sharing stock analyses in several newspapers. In this way, "people will trust you and listen to your analysis." Zeng added, "Some people will search, find, and follow your blog and microblog to obtain your stock commentary after reading your newspaper columns." Gao agreed that he posts his stock commentary online to allow a larger audience to read his commentary, including investors who miss the TV or radio programs, or who do not read the newspapers. All three stock commentators claim that they share very similar main ideas in their stock commentary in the mass media and that which appears on their online platforms. Mr. Gao said that "most of my followers (of the microblog) online are my audience members (from TV programs). It is impossible to say A on TV and B online. People would question my honesty."

At this point, it is easy to assume that the three entities that determine who can be risk definers—the government, the financial corporations, and the mass media outlets—would guarantee the quality of the commentary and commentators for the public, thus minimizing investor uncertainty. However, a professional-oriented risk culture will continue to dominate regardless of whether the individual investors are trading on their own, because overall, they will follow the professional comments made by their selected experts. Interestingly, both the stock commentators and investors reject this presumption.

For the stock commentators, the problem rests with the gate keepers. The people working in mass media, and those with personal connections to media personnel, largely control professional stock analysts' access to the channels through which they may share their analyses. The professional have-mores seek to be recruited by the mass media as stock commentators, with the mass media personnel deciding who will share stock analysis. Here, *guanxi* steps in. Mr. Zeng tells me that in order to become a stock commentator, one requires a strong interpersonal relationship (*guanxi*) with the people in control of the company's referrals (usually the senior managers or the people working in the PR or media departments), the TV producers and program hosts, the newspaper editors, and/or magazine editors. He himself is "like a grandson" to many of his colleagues who recommend him to the media outlets. Zeng declares that he has heard that some finance companies use different approaches—not all of which are that innocent—to develop guanxi with high-ranking mass media managers, a situation that allows employees of certain companies to give stock commentary. Sometimes, the professional have-mores themselves seek out such guanxi with mass media directly, because they desperately need the stock commentator label, and they want to ensure that they can access the mass media to share their stock analyses. The traditional media's role as a gatekeeper to ensure objectivity and professionalism (Livingstone & Bennett, 2003) is shaken under such circumstances.

For the stock commentators, accessing the mass media is not enough. They are faced with threats to be kicked out if they fail to meet requirements from the media's end. If commentators stop sharing stock analyses through the mass media for a while, they are forgotten and will no longer be considered stock commentators. Thus, junior stock commentators like Zeng focus on satisfying the requirements of the mass media in order to ensure that their commentary continues to be shared on TV, newspapers, and in other media forms. These commentators associate the mass media's criteria with high risk.

> You know, as a stock commentator, you can't say whatever you want to say in the media. Take TV programs as an example. There is some censorship from the Publicity Department (*zhongxuanbu*) and Securities Regulatory Commission (*zhengjianhui*) [government censorship]. You have to be careful when commenting on stocks. You can criticize government policies, for example, but not in too radical a way. And the TV programs are concerned about TV ratings, so they like the stock commentators to show a positive attitude towards the market, even if your analysis shows that it will be a bear market. I know investors accuse us of making ambiguous statements. You know what? That's because the TV producers and hosts do not want the stock commentators to be too radical. Also, if your stock commentary is inconsistent with market tendencies too many times, you are out. The TV programs encourage ambiguous comments only if they look very professional, but they do not welcome an inaccurate but clear statement.

Mr. Zeng addressed several concepts regarding stock commentary requirements, including satisfying government censorship, showing optimism, encouraging conservation, demonstrating professionalism, and possessing strong accuracy. Zeng added that the requirements of different mass media may differ slightly. For example, newspapers require commentators to provide a more in-depth analysis to show their professional ability in understanding the long-term tendencies of the market. Adherence to government censorship and moderation is prioritized, even though these conditions conflict with other requirements of a commentator such as professionalism and accuracy. Mr. Gao, a more senior stock commentator, confirmed Zeng's statements. He mentioned that before the 2008 Beijing Olympic Games, stock commentators were discouraged, if not forbidden, to release stock market predictions that were too passive, anything that "would ruin the happy atmosphere ... It's ridiculous. I have to compromise my own analysis, or I will be kicked off of the programs."

Due to such compromises, stock commentators find themselves in an unusually awkward position, caught between the audience and the mass media. On the one hand, they are worried that prioritizing the media's requirements might reduce the accuracy of their comments, harming their reputations as decent risk definers. But on the other hand, to fail the mass media means removal from being a risk definer at all. To deal with this paradox, stock commentators often apply certain strategies.

Mr. Gao, for example, diluted his pessimistic tone before the Olympic events; he simply asked investors to be cautious and stay calm regarding the performance of certain industries. But all in all, he still did not feel good about the situation, because he felt he sometimes sacrificed his professionalism. In other words, he chose the mass media over his followers and audience, because the former determines his status as a famous stock commentator. Almost all of the interviewed stock commentators admitted that they would make the same choice, satisfying mass media regulations over mass investors. As such, publicly shared stock commentary does not accurately reflect the professional have-mores' true analysis of stock quotes and public news. Such commentary is very much devalued in investors' eyes. Mr. Gao shared his dislike of the current relationship between the mass media and stock commentators, regarding it as risky:

> Bad money drives out the good. The really good stock commentators who share decent analyses find it hard to compete with those who kiss the ass of the mass media. Eventually, no one will want to share good analyses. They are busy building up relationships with producers and editors.

Another threat to stock commentators' risk definer positions are the "black mouths" (heizui), those who "ruin the reputations of the stock commentators" (Gao). Zeng stated that these black mouths cheat and manipulate investors by intentionally sharing inaccurate stock commentary:

> The audience's trust in us is crucial. I feel sad that some black mouths are ruining it. They share stock commentary with a purpose. For instance, they share some accurate information of the market to show their professionalism; however, the information they share is not their professional analysis, but the insider information they are told by the bankers. When they win the trust of the audience, they cheat them. For instance, they are told that a banker wants to sell a stock. Then they tell the audience that the stock company is not a desirable target to invest in by misinterpreting the tendencies of the stock prices or the relevant news. When the audience buys in, the banker sells out. I know many black mouths are doing such things. I am afraid my own reputation will be hurt by those guys.

Zeng told me with frustration that some investors have accused him of being a black mouth on his microblog, and he worries that his future career and reputation are in danger, because he's still a rookie who does not have a solid position either in his company or in the mass media. But to be fair, black mouths have existed since the very beginning of stock communication, even back in the "good old days," according to senior commentators, Mr. Gao and Mr. Liang. But the difference is, with the guarantee of government certifications and approval by the mass media, it is difficult to "kick the black mouths out if they are licensed and have a good relationship with the mass media personnel" (Mr. Liang). Back in the 1990s, it was difficult for a black mouth or an incapable stock commentator to stay in the limelight for long. Usually, after publicizing false predictions a few times, people stopped listening, and they could no longer position themselves as stock commentators. During this time, the accuracy of stock commentary was valued more than anything. This situation persuaded stock commentators to deliver stock analysis to the public without revisions and compromises. As Mr. Liang described,

> Back in our time, I was a star in the brokerage firm, because my professional analysis was very accurate. After the opening hours of the market, we investors usually talked about our analysis of the stocks in the stock exchange hall or in the Big Investor Room. If your opinions were sharp and accurate, people would listen to you, and more and more of your listeners would gather in and outside the stock exchange hall. The manager of the brokerage firm thought I could help them attract more clients, so he asked me to give some regular presentations in the stock exchange hall, and some newspapers invited me to write stock commentary. So to speak, the stock commentators at that time were democratically elected by the market and by the other investors who listened to and judged your analysis.

According to Mr. Liang and Gao, back in the 1990s, neither the government nor the mass media decided who was, or was not, an appropriate stock commentator. Instead, the title was given democratically by a large number of investors. Positive investor responses to accurate analyses could boost one's popularity and propel an analyst into the role of stock commentator. Their reputation depended on the size of the crowd encircling them, the willingness of people to listen to their public talks, buy newspapers with their columns, listen to them on the radio, and watch TV for their appearances. As such, investors were not merely audience members, but judges. Should stock comments prove to be inaccurate, investors had the power to strip one's status as a stock commentator by ceasing to receive that person's analysis. For the senior stock commentators, this process was more democratic because investors could freely "elect" (Mr. Liang) the most capable sharers as stock commentators, rather than letting the mass media choose for them. When complaining about the current relationship between the mass media and stock commentators, Mr. Gao told me that he felt respected and comfortable with the media outlets in 1990s. At that time, the media were eager to invite and recruit the most welcomed stock commentators, rather than regulate them with "ridiculous rules" (Gao).

Another difference can be seen in the fact that the new generation of stock commentators mostly come from financial institutions, while the old generation is mostly composed of individual investors—to be more specific, the big ones. They think that their wealth from the stock market indicates professional and accurate market analysis, and such indicators are much better than government certifications. As Gao stated,

> It's simple logic. If you can predict the market correctly, you can make money. Your wealth shows your professionalism. You know what I think when I am invited to give a talk with those young stock commentators? 'You little kids are just small investors. You cannot even make money based on your own analysis. How dare you share your analysis with others!' These new stock commentators gain their positions by kissing the ass of the hosts and the TV producers. Only decent, accurate stock commentary can prove one's professionalism. The certifications gained by those new stock commentators, in my eyes, mean absolutely nothing.

For the senior stock commentators, the current official certifications required by the mass media result from the government's control. They state that in order to regulate the first generation of stock commentators, the government has set up official requirements and examinations. Only those licensed through this system can be labeled as stock commentators. They believe that these certifications lower them to the level of the most incapable stock commentators who pass examinations by memorizing textbooks rather than providing accurate stock commentary. Even worse, some who made really decent stock predictions based on their experiences but lacked certification were expelled from the market, simply because they did not have a relevant educational background. Those who are certified are regarded as professional have-mores who meet the basic requirements of a stock commentator.

Zeng, a junior stock commentator (who is maybe one of the "little kids" in the eyes of Mr. Gao), protests that 1990s stock commentary was a form of dangerous, barbaric, chaotic anarchy: "Who can trust a person who cannot even pass those basic examinations?" But one thing is for sure: Publicly communicated stock commentary in China has become devalued, as reflected in the general mocking tone held by big investors like Mr. Chen.

> How expensive is a newspaper publishing stock commentary? 50 cents, one Yuan, or one Yuan and 50 cents? Ignorant investors want to make big money like us by spending one Yuan and 50 cents. It's a joke. Only in their dreams could they do so. Those (stock commentators) will not tell them anything of value (in their analyses).

Small Investors Taking Back the Position as Evaluator

Though sharply worded, Mr. Chen's argument brings to mind two further issues. We now have heard enough from the experts about communicating stock commentary, including their thoughts regarding the risk arising from or even produced by the current expert system and its evaluation of risk for the general public. The question remains as to how small investors—the majority of whom are professional have-lesses—react to this problematic system of communicating stock commentary? Do they choose to trust this system based on the risk definers of finance, standing side by side with the expert-oriented risk culture? Do they merely follow stock commentary through mass media, making them potential victims of black mouths? The second, more complicated issue is this question: if "one Yuan and 50 cents" cannot buy valuable market analysis, what can?

Regarding the first issue, the small investors have made it very clear to me that they generally lack faith in stock commentary. To deal with the risk in stock commentary, they take such advice with a pinch of salt, and they also develop alternative evaluation systems to replace the current gate keepers. For instance, they rate the stock commentators on their own or with other investors. As Mr. Qian, a small investor, pointed out,

> I am not an idiot, and I would not randomly trust a stock commentator on TV. There are many stock commentators, and many of them are incompetent in making accurate predictions about the market. Even though I don't understand the professional terms that the stock commentators use to explain the market, I understand when they make predictions about the future tendencies of stock prices. Many stock commentators try to blur their conclusions, but they still have to say if the prices will rise or fall. I always investigate a stock commentator and the stock commentary he makes over several weeks and months, comparing his stock comments with the tendencies of the market. If he proves to be accurate, it means his analysis works, and I put him on my trust list.

Qian and many of the interviewed investors say that after making a judgment about a stock commentator, they often share it with their friends or post it online. They are more than happy to attack incapable stock commentators or "black mouths." This rating is casual, as though they were scoring a restaurant on DianPing[1] or rating a hotel on Book.com. Though scattered, the commentary of stock commentators can be found everywhere online, from microblogs to blogs to forums. If one looks up the name of a particular stock commentator or TV program on a search engine, he or she will find many opinions such as "Commentator X is doing a great job! Please keep him on the program" or "Today's (program) is bullshit. Why don't they kick out commentators A and B? They talk nonsense every day, wasting our time."

Stock commentators express a sense of pressure due to this online discourse. Even Gao, a very senior stock analyst who has a good relationship with mass media, is not comfortable with the negative online discourse toward him, especially "when they comment on the official micro-blog account of the (TV) program." It is quite clear that the most welcomed stock commentators receive more attention, which their comments are discussed positively and frequently, while those perceived to be incapable are granted indifference. Those who are labeled as black mouths generate a great deal of discussion like the popular commentators, but the majority of their comments are negative, if not offensive. In this context, non-ICT users like Ms. Li miss the chance to write feedback about the commentators or conveniently gain insight from others' comments. Instead, they have to depend on daily face-to-face conversations with other small investors to learn how people perceive various stock commentators. A typical conversation I have noted from on-site observations in stock exchange halls goes like this: "Is (stock commentator's name) good or bad?" "The one on (program name)? I am not sure. Let me have a look at how netizens think of him."

Meanwhile, the small investors also seek out stock commentary from unlicensed stock commentators, who are not allowed to publicly discuss their analyses and predictions regarding financial investment. These unlicensed individuals usually do not hesitate to voice their radical and clear opinions about the stock market. They use this tactic to attract followers and grow their audience. The shock value differs from the measured analyses of licensed stock commentators, who are forced to make their opinions ambiguous due to mass media pressure and government censorship issues. Small investors support these unlicensed commentators by forwarding their opinions online, joining the commentator's personal chat groups, and even buying memberships from these "suspicious ones," as formal stock analysts and stock commentators call them.

In essence, the investors have developed a new evaluation system online, basing their discussion around stock commentators on different digital platforms. By its very nature, this process has many similarities to the public gathering spaces surrounding stock commentators in the 1990s. In the old days, the more the public gathered around a stock commentator, the more professional the stock commentator would be considered. In the digital era, investors do not gather around the respected commentator physically, but they do use online discourse to express a trusting relationship. In so doing, the investors claim the evaluator position for themselves, snatching it away from the government's license system, financial institutions, and the mass media. Many believe that these three institutions took this power away from the masses at the end of the 1990s, but now, ICT users can fight back.

A New Risk Emerges

With their digital devices, small investors are indeed redefining professionalism. From previous chapters, it has become crystal clear that Western-originated financial knowledge falls short in defining financial risk in China. This understanding requires a specific kind of expertise, a combination of textbook training and local experiences—and some investors even insist the former is unnecessary. Rather, an individual has to have a special sort of intelligence to understand the unique financial risk in China's stock market. He or she must closely observe the separation between economic conditions and market indexes, the distance between a company's conditions and stock quotes, and sudden attacks from government policies. To prove this unique expertise, a commentator must provide accurate predictions, demonstrating a long-term and patterned accuracy that extends beyond one-shot insider information. According to senior stock investors, it was easier to ascertain such accuracy in the 1990s based on a stock commentator's level of wealth. The brokerages and investors did not care so much about privacy issues back then. For example, as discussed in Chapter 3, the investors in the Big Investor Room knew each other's rough investing condition. There were almost no secrets about portfolios. Mr. Liang casually talked about a once big stock commentator and his wealth. He waved his hand when I asked if the two of them were friends because he knew so much about this particular commentator:

> I didn't need to be his friend to know what's in his pocket. He said it. The managers of his brokerage said it. I knew his wealth skyrocketed because of Stock A and B. But he lost a hell a lot of it in mid-1999 because he made a lot of mistakes that year. He still tried to pretend to be a millionaire, but we all knew what he was. The public soon knew what he was. He disappeared eventually.

As Mr. Liang has pointed out, many stock commentators back then even purposely showed off the money they earned in a bull market, and how much they managed to save during a bear market. In this way, they could build up trust between them and the small investors, attracting a larger audience. Their trading performance spoke louder than anything else.

In the government license era, wealth fails to be an effective criterion for evaluating stock commentators. The license mechanism perpetuated by the government, financial institutions/companies, and mass media has replaced the democratic evaluation system maintained by the public. In this context, investors are physically separated from mass media stock commentators. They are able to obtain a commentator's affiliation, as introduced by the host of a program (e.g. Mr. or Ms. A, a stock analyst from finance company B). In other words, investors are separated from experts through physical space and by personal information. For instance, they cannot learn about the experts' wealth conditions and portfolio investments. By its very nature, the license system institutionalizes stock commentators, persuading the once individual risk definer to be employed by the finance companies. The government exercises discipline on stock analysis—so many accountants and institutional stock analysts cannot invest for themselves if they want to avoid insider information problems. Therefore, people judge the performance of a financial institution rather than the pockets of a personal commentator. However, when a stock commentator's ability becomes part of an institution's expertise, the commentator's level of accuracy inevitably becomes diluted. Mr. Huang, a small investor, points out that it's "hard to tell" an institutional stock commentator's true expertise nowadays:

> You don't know if it is the analyst who is good. Maybe his predictions are right because the team is good … Maybe the analyst is just being used as an advertisement (for the financial company) without any true abilities.

To compete with the dominant expert system and legitimate stock commentators in the digital media space, unlicensed commentators usually claim to work on their own—or contribute the most to a team. This means their analysis and predictions are their own. To prove the strength of their predictions, they "have no shame" (Mr. Liang); they show off their money, and many of them show their followers screenshots of their investing accounts as proof of their accuracy. These commentators have a common trick: They use blogs or microblogs to publicize their stock analyses, and they ask their followers to join them in private chat rooms. The investors have to pay different membership levels to join in various chat rooms. Some say that the more you pay the stock commentator, the more accurate and detailed the information. The stock commentators usually make money by selling such memberships, or they even manipulate the market like a banker by releasing false information in different chat rooms. Mr. Liang, a professional stock commentator, used contempt to describe how unlicensed commentators "play the game":

> For example, he (the unlicensed stock commentator) has three groups in three chatrooms. He releases bull news to Group A first, which is the core group. He and group A members are bottom fishing the stock first, and then release the bull news to Group B and Group C. Group B and Group C have more members, but they pay a lower membership fee. With the two groups' support, the targeted company's price goes up temporarily, which makes his prediction look accurate. Eventually, he and Group A members become the

only winners. It's two-bit. It's disgusting to see how the followers kiss the ass of the cheaters, calling them "teachers."

The membership fee that small investors pay to unlicensed stock commentators is their answer to Mr. Chen's declaration that "one Yuan and 50 cents (the price of a financial newspaper) cannot buy decent stock analysis." Such membership fees are not regarded as commissions to a fund manager, because they are not based upon a contractual relationship at all, even an informal form. To understand Mr. Liang's "kiss ass" and "teacher" comments, it is necessary to note another phenomenon: Small investors try to build up a social relationship (guanxi) with unlicensed stock commentators using online platforms. These small investors are keenly aware that the cyber membership promises them nothing; there is no guarantee from the government or the legitimate expert system. To overcome such uncertainties, they seek guanxi with these "teachers," hoping that a more intimate social relationship will grant them more accurate stock predictions in private.

This risk culture of the small investors goes beyond China's expert system, allowing them to choose a risk definer based upon guanxi instead of contract while communicating stock commentary privately rather than publicly. The professional have-mores can't understand why investors turn to a blogger or microblogger from nowhere rather than listen to experienced, professional, and governmentally licensed experts from formal media outlets. Many interviewed experts used one case, the "Daitoudage777" crisis, to prove the absurdity of small investors following an outsider instead of them. In Chinese, Daitoudage means "the big brother who leads you." In 2005 and 2006, he was an active user on online stock discussion forums. This Daitoudage person (whose real name is Xiujie Wang) used his blogs to post a great deal of commentary regarding stocks and the market. His commentary appeared on NetEase and Sina,[2] two leading e-service companies that provide popular social media services in China. Some of his main predictions differed from the mainstream opinion given by official stock commentators, but they seemed to align with the overall tendency of the market. Daitoudage was not shy when showing off his market prediction abilities. In a blog posted on January 26, 2006, he said the following:

> The stock index started to surge in 2006, in a way that the majority of people did not understand … At the beginning of the Spring Festival, I said that the index would reach 1300 points, and many of my friends mocked me and said that I was out of my mind. Now it seems that it is not me who has lost his mind. At the beginning of this year, I especially recommended 600489, 600547, 600497, 600432, and 600549 (stock codes), and all of their prices have surged strongly,

even better than my prediction of increases of 50% each. In the short term, it seems there is a high probability that these securities will start dropping in price ... Please watch out, guys.[3]

We can see from this excerpt that Daitoudage, like other unlicensed stock commentators, made straightforward predictions about the market and specific securities, making him stand out from the cautious licensed commentators providing ambiguous stock commentary. This bold strategy attracted many online followers. Daitoudage was particularly popular among all the unlicensed commentators, perhaps because he portrayed himself as a Robinhood-like professional have-more. He claimed that he once worked for famous finance companies and brokerages (all of which proved false), and that he could be more honest and frank than licensed experts. In his blog entitled, "My Opinion about Five Big Financial Institutions who Make Stock Commentary," he attacked the licensed expert system while flattering himself in an intelligent manner:

The first one is Beijing Shoufang.[4] Their skills are quite bad, yet their attitude about making apologies is nice ... They are always one step behind the market. Yesterday they screamed that today the stock index would drop, and this morning, when the market boomed, they immediately changed their opinion during the noon commentary, saying that they think the index will increase ... Shenyin Wanguo Securities,[5] their technical analysis is decent..., but they are being too conservative, lacking the fresh air of youth. This is where I came from, so I hope they will rise to the occasion and be their best again ... As for Guotai Junan Securities,[6] their techniques are declining; however, their analysis of the fundamentals is special ... too conservative ... Finally, there is the China International Capital Corporation.[7] Years before, these (experts) coming from overseas were okay, but now they are only good at predicting the rating mechanism ... After two years, I think they will lose their core ability as well.

Daitoudage's spicy online critiques of these dominant brokerages and finance companies somehow resonated with small investors who distrusted the expert system. Of course, his comments were not necessarily true, but the sanhu no longer cared. After winning the trust of the small investors, he persuaded his followers to buy memberships to his private chat rooms for more detailed commentary. Shockingly, Daitoudage's blog had received over 30 million clicks by the time he was arrested in 2007 for illegal business dealings. After his release, he began posting blogs again, and in one of his last posts on NetEase, he even commented on the U.S. presidential election of 2016. He was as bold as ever, but the acuity of his former predictions seemed to have disappeared:

If Trump wins, then the price of gold will surge like crazy. Between one and one-thirty pm (Chinese time), the U.S. presidential election will probably be decided. If Trump is elected, the Chinese stock index will drop below 3100 points, and then increase drastically. The price of gold will increase dramatically as well. If Hilary wins, (the price) will surge directly. I hope Trump will win and beat that witch.[8]

Diverging from his prediction, however, the Shanghai Stock Index ended at 3,128 points on November 9, 2016, dropping 0.62% that day. The licensed experts and supervising actors were not surprised by these numbers. However, what to the surprise of them is that small investors continue to follow unlicensed commentators, even after Daitoudage's arrest. People have found other "teachers" to listen to, paying for chat room memberships to improve their chances of success. A more recent scandal involves one of these "teachers" using photo editing software to fake screenshots of her investing account. She put up a photo online as she had several times before, declaring that she had predicted the market right and earned a lot of money from her portfolio. However, someone soon pointed out that the stock codes on the picture were just not right. She disappeared soon after she was caught in her lie.

The professional have-mores look at it as a joke, confirming once again that small investors seek information from outside the expert system out of ignorance and greed. But Mr. Qin, a small investor, offers a different perspective. He still believes that Daitoudage had some true ability in evaluating financial risk, even though it turned out that he had almost no educational background in finance. His argument summarizes the logic of the online risk culture developed by small investors: They insist that there should be alternatives to the current system, which produces just as much as uncertainty for investors, if not more.

> It's not like we (small investors) are dumb. We know how risky it is (to follow an unlicensed stock commentator online). The Internet is full of liars. But it would not be better to trust a stock commentator. At least the unlicensed ones are more frank, while the stock comments on TV are ambiguous. I can compare their straightforward predictions with the market tendencies. I can be cautious. If something goes wrong, I withdraw … The issue is, I don't feel protected by the license system. I don't feel protected by a contract with a fund.

Notes

1 A popular restaurant rating platform in China.
2 Daitoudage777's blog on NetEase can be seen here: http://dtdg777.blog.163. com/. He stopped to update the NetEase blog since 2016. For his blog on Sina, he used to use this http://blog.sina.com.cn/u/1177358635 address to post his

blogs, but now he used the blog here http://blog.sina.com.cn/u/3237746222. Though he continued to write blogs, his recent posts received much less clicks and subscribers than his old posts.

3 The original blog is available here: http://dtdg777.blog.163.com/blog/static/ 2477207220060263521342/

4 Beijing Shoufang was once a famous investing firm in China. However, its chairman, Jianzhong Wang, was involved in the financial criminal and being investigated by CSRC in 2008. He was suspected to buy in several stocks first, recommend the listed companies of which to the public in name of Beijing Shoufang, and making profits when the investors believed in their evaluations and invest in the stocks. In 2011, Wang was convicted of manipulation of market.

5 Shenyin Wanguo Securities is one of the leading brokerage firms and finance companies in China. Daitoudage777 declared that he used to work for the brokerage, which was denied by the brokerage staff who said "never heard of this person working here." See the relevant news report for reference: http://finance.people.com.cn/GB/42774/5971484.html

6 Guotai Junan Securities, like Shenyin Wanguo Securities, is also one of the largest and leading finance companies in China, whose business includes stock brokerage and financial investment.

7 China International Capital Corporation is mostly well known as "Zhongjin Company" in China. It is the first joint-venture investment bank in China, launched in 1995.

8 See http://dtdg777.blog.163.com/blog/static/2477207220161091158444/

References

Dominick, J. R. (2010). *The dynamics of mass communication: Media in the digital age.* New York: Tata McGraw-Hill Education.

Livingston, S., & Bennett, W. L. (2003). Gatekeeping, indexing, and live-event news: Is technology altering the construction of news? *Political Communication, 20*(4), 363–380.

Conclusion

As we come to a close, it is a good time to look back at the complexity of risk communication in China's financial world. The "risk" to be communicated includes the uncertainties regarding the listed company, the industry, or the national market as a whole. To form an opinion, investors require various information like stock quotes, company news, financial statements, national policies, international news, and different expert commentary and analysis. At this point, the second type of risk emerges—not in the uncertainties of the portfolio or the market but in the communication process for evaluating such uncertainties. The most convincing definer of financial risk will be the one who not only nails predictions but also demonstrates greater confidence and security in communicating such information.

In markets dominated by a professional-oriented risk culture, professional elites are the dominant, if not the only, risk definers in finance. Most people excuse themselves from risk communication ostensibly because they have faith in the expert system—the government, the accounting firms, the law firms, the banks, the finance companies, and the experts in general. They believe that such experts are able to handle financial risk. As mentioned in Chapter 1, however, they are unable to challenge the dominance of the professional institutions and individuals in defining risk even when they start to question the system's ability to do this job or when they begin to raise an eyebrow over the social inequalities inherent in the power hierarchies of finance. This paradox rests on the fact that they themselves face major uncertainty in evaluating financial risk on their own. More specifically, their uncertainty arises from two areas: difficulties in conveniently and cheaply obtaining the most up-to-date information (e.g. stock quotes and financial statements), and a lack of professional knowledge supposedly able to scientifically transform uncertainty into security. Even though there exists competition between risk definer positions in finance, this competition is an internal battle within the expert system (e.g. finance companies pointing fingers at the government experts, or the government instituting laws and regulations on the markets and financial institutions). The scattered majority, or "nobs" in the eyes of financial experts, are rather far removed from the risk communication process.

In China, it is a different story. The stock market was born within a society in transition, embracing capitalism but still holding onto the ideal of socialism. This marriage of apparent contradictions means two things: the financial markets in China face an extremely strong government with a socialist spirit at heart, and a general public that remains somehow committed to social equality. Allowing the general public, whether rich or poor, to participate in the financial game seemed to be the righteous and only option once upon a time. The major actors in finance were not unhappy with this "the more the merrier" mentality. The government, for example, wanted an active and energetic market, and the financial institutions, including brokerages, sought more commissions from customers. It benefited everyone to make the stock investment communication process more egalitarian to align with the interests of different social groups. Coincidentally, the growth of China's stock market was accompanied by the rapid development of information and communication technologies (ICTs) in the 1990s. Like seeds placed into fertile soil, ICTs bore the fruits of numerous Chinese media platforms able to facilitate stock investment communication.

But allowing the majority to participate in the game does not necessarily mean that government authorities want the masses to have a risk definer position. For the government, individual and institutional big investors could become manipulators, with small investors being vulnerable and ignorant, causing chaos in the markets. Thus, the government is obliged to dominate risk communication for the public good, and they do so with national policies and securities regulations—or by simply voicing an opinion regarding financial risk through mass media, keeping both the big and small investors at bay. However, as society continued to clash with the growing capitalist markets, it became apparent that a purely government-led risk culture would not work well in the financial world. One typical example occurred in the 1990s when people became devoted to stock commentators (instead of the government), seeking their opinions and risk evaluations. There were also complaints about sudden attacks on the markets due to government policies from time to time. The government then changed its position into a commander or ruler, supporting a regulated expert system to become frontline risk definers. Through a certification mechanism, the individual stock commentators, many of whom were big investors at that time, became institutionalized through various finance companies (several interviewees used the term "amnesty" to describe such institutionalization process). Some who did not adapt to the new system were expelled from their dominant position in risk communication—the government-controlled mass media outlets would no longer allow them to voice stock commentary.

However, a professional-dominated risk culture has failed to flourish in China, even with support from the government, mass media outlets, and finance companies. If we look back at previous chapters, the main reason is clear: the current expert system has failed to win the trust of the general public (including many experts themselves). The core of a professional-oriented risk culture is security based on systematic knowledge, the idea that the professional have-mores have an upper hand in analyzing and predicting uncertainties compared to professional have-lesses. Indeed, this idea has dislodged the general public from the more mature financial markets. But China has unique social conditions with a powerful government devaluing if not dismantling professionalism, particularly because the liberal theories and formulas for risk evaluation become fragile when facing dominant policy makers. A second blow to professionalism is the social corruption in China: people gain privileges through their personal relationships (*guanxi*). Real or imagined, the guanxi among the listed companies, media outlets, government officials, accounting firms, and law firm has corroded the public trust in the company information. In Chapter 1, I have mentioned that one crucial promise of stock markets to our societies is that good firms obtain the money they need to expand and promote. The issue in China is that only the very insiders know whether a company is decent or not. Unable to gain security via making sense of the public information by professional knowledge, the big investors position themselves as bankers in a gambling game, using their capital to develop guanxi themselves. They either manipulate the markets through corrupted experts or mass media, or obtain insider information to take advantage of small investors, earning a quick buck before being caught by the government.

Small investors in China are very aware of the risk arising from these conditions. They thus play a role in risk communication, with their ICT devices in hand. They take control of communicating stock quotes, news, and trading orders themselves. They follow a swift process regardless of excessive speculation, instead of trusting a corrupt finance company for long-term investment. They try to learn some basic financial knowledge to evaluate risk on their own, or they discuss investments with other small potatoes online and offline as backup. But when such communication does not work for certain information (e.g. financial statements), the uncertainties become too great, and the small investors have to turn to the expert system for help. The small investors then try not only to evaluate the regulated and legitimate system represented in mass media but also to select their own risk definers through the Internet. When sensing corrupt public information, they also seek to develop guanxi online for more accurate predictions of future markets.

Ostensibly, the big and small investors reinforce a barbarian and unprofessional guanxi-oriented risk culture in markets, which creates risk not only for themselves but also for the whole financial market. This culture favors speculation over long-term investment, guanxi over contractual relations, and private (if not insider) information over public messages. It nourishes zero-sum relations in finance, one in which one person's security comes at the expense of another's uncertainty. The experts and government may be easy to blame for the irrational behavior and risk-seeking, making China's stock markets a casino. But if people look at the communication process producing and reproducing this culture, they will find that every step of the investors' practice is rational and calculated, seeking security instead of uncertainty. Especially for small investors, staying in the communication process is risky. The problem is that they would be more vulnerable if they were excluded from the risk definition system (regardless of big brother or big capital control) altogether. That's why they stay in the game and hold onto their ICT devices, a decision that could be viewed as a soft protest against the legitimate risk definers.

This book is being written at a time when China's financial markets are undergoing an uncertain transition process. Therefore, researchers interested in this topic will want to keep an eye on what's happening globally and locally in order to understand the potential impacts on financial communication and risk cultures in China. The war between the guanxi-oriented risk culture and the expert-oriented one is far from over. One phenomenon that could have major implications for this battle is globalization, an inevitable process that continues to clash with the comparatively closed stock markets of China. Economically speaking, not a single entity on earth can completely separate itself from the world. An economically "splendid isolation" would end up anything but splendid nowadays. Even with its extraordinary domestic demand, high population numbers, and authoritarian political regime, China cannot escape the spider web of growingly intense global connections. Although the relationships between economic entities are close, global reflections on local economic performance remain delayed and latent, except during certain critical moments of crises. For instance, this interdependence becomes apparent when markets crash or surge. In the digital media age, a crisis or surge (crisis in particular) is mediated swiftly if not instantly, somehow enhancing or enlarging the local markets' reaction to the distant entity's performance. A particular example is the "rollercoaster" week of the U.S. stock markets in February 2018. On February 5, the Dow Jones industrial average suffered a black Monday closing down at 1,175 points (4.6%) for the day, the largest point drop in Dow history. The markets bounced back a bit, but days later, on February 9, Thursday of the same week, the Dow plummeted again to 1,033 points (4.2%).[1] It is no surprise that such a "crazy week" triggered panic in financial entities that are open and have a close relationship with the United States, including the Tokyo Stock Market in Japan, the Hong Kong Stock Market, and stock markets throughout Europe. What was surprising, though, was how China's stock markets responded to these crashes. Due to the 12-hour time difference between New York and Shanghai, Chinese investors received the news about the

U.S. markets suffering an extraordinary drop quite late. Panic first burst out from professionals who observed the global markets for reference on a daily basis. The licensed and unlicensed stock commentators and analysts started to discuss the crashes, predicting (most of them negatively) how A-share would respond to Dow. The large number of followers for these expert accounts spread the news and commentary with increasing urgency, regardless of the fact that the A-share market was just about to bounce back from a recent plunge. Worry and fear on social media reached its peak around 9 am, when small investors who missed the news during the night woke up and surfed Internet news through apps and social media platforms. In response to market concerns, the Shanghai Composite Index sharply dropped 3% that day, and the trend worsened on Friday of the same week. The benchmark Shanghai Composite Index closed 4.05% lower at 3,129.85 points, and the Shenzhen Composite Index slumped 3.58% to close at 10,001.23 points.[2] Chinese media openly ascribed the sharp plummet in the local stock markets to the Dow's drop.[3] In March 2018, the same situation repeated itself when U.S. president Donald Trump threatened to impose tariffs on Chinese imports. The Dow Jones industrial average plunged 724.42 points to close at 23,957.89 on March 22, with the market fearing the uncertain relationship with China. Indeed, it seemed that there was now an emerging China-United States trade dispute (some observers have used the term "trade war"). Imagine what would have happened if the Chinese political regime still held the dominant and absolute risk position in financial communication: it definitely would have celebrated the sharp drop of the "enemy" market with a surge of its own. What happened instead was panic once again. Fear pervaded the social media environment after receiving the news of the U.S. market crash, and the A-share dropped over 3% due to the tension caused by the trade dispute. The Shanghai and Shenzhen stock markets soon started to surge again when the trade war cooled down a little bit, and the Chinese and American governments joined in discussions together.

In Chapter 4, we noted that international news fails to have much impact on China's financial communication compared to news about national affairs. This situation is changing.

Moreover, China's financial markets have become not only informationally but also mechanically more connected to the world financial system. I discussed the continuously increasing numbers and quotas for foreign finance companies investing in China's stock market under the scheme of Qualified Foreign Institutional Investors (QFII). Though the overall impact on China's stock markets of these foreign financial institutions, capitally or communicatively speaking, remains limited, the situation could change in the future, particularly if the Chinese government decides to further open its financial markets to the world. Compared with QFII, a more fundamental phenomenon occurring in the financial world can be seen in "Connects" programs. Since 2014, China and Hong Kong have launched the so-called Shanghai-Hong Kong and Shenzhen-Hong Kong Stock Connect, facilitating a cross-boundary investment channel for global investors. Mainland China investors thus can invest in a number of Hong Kong securities, and vice versa. Years later, the channel is running stably and smoothly, with billions of dollars being traded on a daily basis. Meanwhile, another giant program, the Shanghai-London Stock Connect, is being negotiated. The deepening of globalization and rising number of collaborations between China's financial markets and the globe may grant Western financial institutions more convincing roles as risk definers in China's stock market. Indeed, the Chinese investors who were interested in the Shanghai- and Shenzhen-Hong Kong Connects told me that they definitely consider the multinational investing banks' released reports when making sense of their stock quotes. Ms. Yu, a stock analyst, told me,

> Well, I am not saying they (the global finance companies) are doing their jobs better than us (the local experts). I am still convinced that we know the Chinese markets better than they do. But you see, the Hong Kong market is extremely sensitive to the reports of those big investing banks. A negative evaluation from the most influential ones can crash a stock easily. We have had to take that into consideration.

Due to ICTs, these reports from the big finance banks are released and mass communicated swiftly, enlarging their impact on the market. Rapidly rising risk definers like Goldman Sachs, UBS AG, and JP Morgan in the Western finance companies have become more and more vocal in China. In the near future, it is my opinion that the local stock commentators, licensed or unlicensed, will still be active communicators delivering "cooked" stock information. But what will happen when the global finance companies compete head to head with them using their advantages in professionalism, with small investors on social media acting as the ultimate evaluators of these risk definers? Is it possible that such competition will allow the expert-oriented risk culture to dominate the future power dynamics of financial communication?

Researchers should continue to observe China's financial world for the long haul if they seek to answer such questions. Indeed, they should pay particular attention to investor attitudes and the Chinese government. Based on the interview data, it is safe to say that the small investors in China admired the professionalism, global view, and comparatively independent position of the global finance companies; however, they took the analysis that these companies communicated with a pinch of salt. "For me, they (the global finance companies) are no different than the (local) big bankers, if they are allowed to get into China's markets with full power," a small investor said to me. He showed me a piece of news online using his smartphone, news stating that a famous investing bank thought a security in China was "overpriced" because the company's latest merging strategy did not look very promising.

> We netizens can check the investing details of these big investors, you know. Many small investors have already found out that the same bank sneakily bought the same security last week. You see this post, and this one…And after one week they say it's overpriced? Don't treat us like fools. We (Chinese small investors) have been 'trained' by the local bankers many times.

Clearly, the global finance companies are not facing a bunch of naïve or drifting masses. Manipulative though they might be, they are simultaneously observing the leading figures of the global financial world with cautious eyes, using their experiences with the local market and their information gained from cyberspace. It's not possible to hold a dominant risk definer position without convincing these picky evaluators.

Moreover, even if these finance institutions with big names win the trust of the local investors, the level of their influence in financial communication remains largely in the hands of the Chinese government. Based upon the rise of Connects programs and the loosening of QFII restrictions, it appears that the Communist Party is taking a quite open attitude toward China's financial markets. However, to encourage openness is one thing, but to accept all of the impacts of openness is another. Would the government accept one foreseeable impact, allowing foreign or international financial experts to seize a powerful risk definer position with regard to financial communication in China? Would they allow foreigners to express their financial opinions loudly, eventually gaining more local followers on social media than the government-licensed experts and local regimes? Would they tolerate, for example, an online report from Goldman Sachs triggering major reactions from the financial community like it does in other markets? From the point of view of a strong government with socialism as its core value, it could be too great a risk to let uncontrollable institutions or individuals from the capitalist world to play such an important role in their own financial world.

But this does not mean that the Chinese government has given up on generating an expert-oriented risk culture in finance. All in all, China has passed its first stage of financial development, during a period when it needed a the-more-the-merrier attitude toward participation in the financial markets. Enthusiasm from scattered individuals used to be the driving force of the markets, but now they can cause trouble, making the market more chaotic. From the point view of efficiency and state stability, it is in the government's interests to let a small group of elites evaluate financial risk for the public. This system makes it easier for the government to control the market while making sure that the state-owned capital remains safe. The issue is what kind of experts they want to be the major communicators. Apparently, the liberalists and foreign experts are big no-no's, because they are out of the government's control. At most, these institutions and individuals are allowed to play less important roles like evaluating global risk and chance for the Chinese audience, though the political regime could change direction in the future. If the political structure maintains the status quo, a government-oriented expert system will still be the party's best choice. As previous chapters illustrate, however, this expert system has faced confrontations from time to time, its honesty has been questioned, and its ability has been the subject of great scrutiny. To encourage this expert system to gain back the dominant risk definer position, it seems that the government must fight the guanxi-based, insider information risk culture that has taken root in China. Only this kind of action could promote public trust toward government-oriented elites. As this book has discussed, these elites can be divided into two groups. The first group includes completely official elites represented by the China Securities Regulatory Commission (CSRC), Shanghai Stock Exchange (SSE), Shenzhen Stock Exchange (SZSE), various levels of law enforcement, the central bank, and other economic and financial-related government departments. These institutions primarily play two roles in financial communication, namely, supervisor and policy maker. To convince the public of their legitimacy, they have made great effort to enhance the supervisory system and reduce corruption issues. They have not hesitated to promote such efforts on their official social media accounts, seeking to convince the public of their trustworthiness. Some of the most mediated topics online include, but are not limited to, the gradual adoption of the delisting stock mechanism, improvements in law enforcement for listed companies and other social organs, and the increased transparency of financial information. Despite the clear determination of the Chinese government in improving its official expert system, it still takes time to win back the public's trust as a supervisor. And the government must consider another obstacle to the official expert system: the ultimate disconnect between an anything but liberalist government and the financial markets. To claim and convince the public of their own expertise in finance, they have to develop more mature and patterned theories to support their economic and financial policies, countering the public belief that these policies are purely artificial.

And this strategy is not only for themselves but also for another group in the government-oriented expert system: licensed experts like fund managers and stock commentators. Public reaction to the financial communication taking place in the 1990s proved that the government "can't have it all." When considering the financial evaluation work of the market or a specific security, the political regime has to take a step back, sharing some risk definition work with the nongovernment expert system. These professional individuals and institutions have a certain level of autonomy, yet they still fall under the supervision of the government. On the one hand, they are the victims of the guanxi-oriented risk culture, losing territory to unlicensed "experts" who communicate stock analysis online. On the other hand, they became the very creators of this risk culture. They are not able to surpass their market competitors with traditional financial expertise. Failing to interpret or predict the policies of an extremely strong government or information from a bunch of corrupt companies, they have acted as market manipulators, bribers, or "black mouths," using their capital or discursive impact to ensure their own security. This sense of security, however, is extremely vulnerable because it comes at the price of small investors' uncertainty. It also costs the experts their legitimacy, fame, and stability, removing them from the promising risk definer positions. The public neither wants to entrust their money to these experts, nor do they want to listen to them blindly, unless developing personal guanxi. Some of the small investors would rather check the comments from unlicensed commentators online. For the time being, it might be possible to "terrify" these experts using stricter law enforcement, but it would not change the situation completely. To persuade the expert-oriented risk culture, the key issue is to generate a new mechanism of professionalism. Let the professionals—and the small investors—feel that expertise works in China, granting them more security in the financial world than insider information. And both the experts and the government need to face the challenge posed by cyberspace. The mass of small investors has the desire and even the ability to select and evaluate the expert system using their own criteria instead of government licenses or mass media and institutional recommendations. Chaotic though it seems, if the small investors, government, finance companies, and traditional and new media systems can reach agreement on a new common ground for selecting and evaluating the expert system, China could open a new "socialist" possibility to the world of global finance, the idea that the general public can join in the financial world and financial communication in a more equal and democratic way than most entities rooted in professionalism. A new risk culture in finance would be generated, one that is either elite-dominated or based upon unreliable if not illegal personal relations. Such a culture would share a social consensus about the future direction of a security in particular and the economy at large.

All that being said, the government can save itself a great deal of trouble by taking another easy road to achieve absolute discursive power in financial communication. As of this book's writing, some experts publicly have been persuading the government to expel small investors from the investment communication process for a safer, more stable, and institution-controlled market. Regarding the online discourse of these "radical" and unprofessional investors, the solution is also very simple. The relevant departments could increase the level of cyber censorship—which has proven effective in controlling social discourse—and reduce if not eliminate the participation of small investors. Simultaneously, they could silence the unlicensed stock commentators from the Internet by shutting down their social media and chat room accounts, removing competitors to the licensed expert system in a clear-cut manner. But a question remains: Is the exclusion of small investors the only answer? And will this exclusion really bring security to the big investors, the listed companies, and the government? Indeed, are the small investors with ICTs really the trouble makers? Are they the ones to blame for the fact that the financial markets often fail to deliver their promises to Chinese society? I believe that the government and the public need to take a closer look at the communication practices of the investors. Only in so doing can they truly understand the risk culture of China's financial world—and make improvements to it.

To end this book, I would like to mention one of the most impressive sights I experienced during my fieldwork for this project. On one of those days—a very ordinary one—I sat with Mr. Huang, a small investor, in the stock exchange hall. It was 3:30 pm, and the stock markets had just closed. Mr. Huang said goodbye to everyone he knew in the hall. He suddenly turned to me and said,

> Hey, you have been to the U.S. and Europe, right? Do you think the *laobaixing* (general public) there experience what we Chinese *laobaixing* do? I doubt it. I guess it's so-called socialism with Chinese characteristics…I still have faith in our society, and in this market, too. It's part of my life.

Notes

1 For reader's reference, the relevant reports about Dow's unusual crash can be seen on Bloomberg www.bloomberg.com/news/articles/2018-02-05/bad-day-turns-terrifying-as-dow-suffers-worst-point-plunge-ever, *the Economic Times* https://economictimes.indiatimes.com/markets/stocks/asia-stocks-pummelled-by-fresh-wall-street-slide-safe-havens-in-demand/articleshow/62844282.cms, and *the Guardian* www.theguardian.com/business/live/2018/feb/08/markets-fall-back-ftse-dow-jones-bank-of-england-interest-rate-decision-business?page=with%3Ablock-5a7cb9e9e4b0365be51684f3

2 The data have been retrieved from the Shanghai and Shenzhen Stock Exchange database.

3 See www.xinhuanet.com/fortune/2018-02/07/c_1122378453.htm and http://finance.huanqiu.com/gjcx/2018-02/11589616.html

Index